First World War
and Army of Occupation
War Diary
France, Belgium and Germany

23 DIVISION
Headquarters, Branches and Services
Adjutant and Quarter-Master General
8 March 1915 - 24 July 1917

WO95/2170/1

The Naval & Military Press Ltd
www.nmarchive.com
Published in association with The National Archives

Published by

The Naval & Military Press Ltd

Unit 10 Ridgewood Industrial Park,
Uckfield, East Sussex,
TN22 5QE England
Tel: +44 (0) 1825 749494

www.naval-military-press.com

www.nmarchive.com

This diary has been reprinted in facsimile from the original. Any imperfections are inevitably reproduced and the quality may fall short of modern type and cartographic standards.

© **Crown Copyright**
Images reproduced by permission of The National Archives, London, England, 2015.

Contents

Document type	Place/Title	Date From	Date To
Heading	WO95/2170/1		
Heading	23rd Division "A" &"O" Branch. Aug 1915-1917 Jly To 1 July Nov. 1917		
Heading	H.Q. 23rd Division A & Q Aug-Oct 1915 vol 1 121/7595		
Heading	War Diary Headquarters 23rd Division A.A.& M.G.Branch August 1915.		
Heading	War Diary Headquarters 23rd. Division. A.A. & Q.M.G. Branch. August 1915.		
War Diary	Bordon	20/08/1915	25/08/1915
War Diary	Folkestone	25/08/1915	25/08/1915
War Diary	Boulogne	25/08/1915	26/08/1915
War Diary	Tilques	26/08/1915	31/08/1915
Heading	War Diary Headquarters 23rd. Division. A.A.& Q.M.G. branch. September 1915.		
War Diary	Tilques	31/08/1915	06/09/1915
War Diary	Renescure	06/09/1915	07/09/1915
War Diary	Merria	07/09/1915	16/09/1915
War Diary	Croix Du Bac	16/09/1915	02/10/1915
Heading	War Diary Headquarters 23rd. Division. A.A.& Q.M.G. Branch.October 1915.		
War Diary	Croix du Bac	01/10/1915	31/10/1915
Heading	H.Q. 23rd for A. & Q. Vol:2 121/7635 Nov 15		
War Diary	Croix Du Bac	01/11/1915	01/12/1915
Heading	A&Q. 23rd Div Vol:3 121/7936		
Heading	War Diary A&Q.Branch. 23rd Division December 1915		
War Diary	Croix Du Bac	01/12/1915	31/12/1915
Heading	23rd Div. A & Q January to December 1816		
Heading	A&Q. 23rd Div vol:4		
War Diary	Croix Du Bac	01/01/1916	09/02/1916
Heading	A&Q. 23rd Div. vol 5		
War Diary	Croix Du Bac	10/02/1916	23/02/1916
War Diary	Croix Du Bac & Estaires	24/02/1916	24/02/1916
War Diary	Estaires	25/02/1916	25/02/1916
War Diary	Estaires & Blaringhem	26/02/1916	26/02/1916
War Diary	Blaringhem	27/02/1916	28/02/1916
War Diary	Blaringhem & Bruay	29/02/1916	29/02/1916
Heading	A & Q. 23 D W Vol 6		
War Diary	Bruay	01/03/1916	07/03/1916
War Diary	Ch de la Haie	08/03/1915	10/03/1915
War Diary	Chateau de La Haie	11/03/1916	15/03/1916
War Diary	Bruay	16/03/1915	21/03/1915
War Diary	Sains en Gohelle	22/03/1915	31/03/1915
Heading	War Diary "A" "Q" Branch 23rd Division 1st April to 30th April		
War Diary	Sains en Gohelle	01/04/1915	18/04/1915
War Diary	Bruay	19/04/1915	30/04/1915
Heading	War Diary A & D Branch 23rd Division 1st May 1916 to 31st May 1916 Volume IX		
War Diary	Bruay	09/05/1915	12/05/1915

War Diary	Sains En Gohelle	13/04/1915	19/04/1915
War Diary	Gohelle	20/04/1915	28/04/1915
War Diary	Sains en Gohelle	28/05/1915	28/05/1915
War Diary	Barlin	29/05/1915	31/05/1915
Heading	A & Q 23 DW Vol 9 War Diary A & Q Branch 23rd Division 1st January 1916 to 30th June 1916		
War Diary	Barlin	01/06/1916	05/06/1916
War Diary	Gohelle	06/06/1916	13/06/1916
War Diary	Bruay	14/06/1916	19/06/1916
War Diary	Bomy	16/06/1916	23/06/1916
War Diary	Vauxen Amienois	24/06/1916	30/06/1916
Heading	A & Q 23rd Divn July 1916		
Heading	War Diary A&Q Branches 23rd division 1st July 1916 to 31st July 1916		
War Diary	Vauxen Amienois	01/07/1916	01/07/1916
War Diary	Baizieux	02/07/1916	03/07/1916
War Diary	Vivier Mill	03/07/1916	10/07/1916
War Diary	St.Gratien	11/07/1916	20/07/1916
War Diary	Henencourt	21/07/1916	25/07/1916
War Diary	Albert	26/07/1916	28/07/1916
War Diary	D 27 C 55 Sheet 57D	29/07/1916	31/07/1916
Heading	23rd Division A & Q. 23rd Division August 1916		
Heading	War Diary A&Q Branches 23rd Division 1 August 1916 to 31 August 1916		
War Diary	Camp W27C6 Sheet 57d	01/08/1916	07/08/1916
War Diary	Baizieux	08/08/1916	10/08/1916
War Diary	Ailly Le Haut Clocher	11/08/1916	12/08/1916
War Diary	Fletre	13/08/1916	16/08/1916
War Diary	Steenwerck	17/08/1916	28/08/1916
War Diary	Bailleul	29/08/1916	31/08/1916
Heading	War Diary A and Q Branches 23rd Division 1 September 1916 to 30 September 1916 Vol XIII		
War Diary	Bailleul	01/09/1916	05/09/1916
War Diary	Tilques	06/09/1916	10/09/1916
War Diary	Allonville	11/09/1916	11/09/1916
War Diary	Baizieux	12/09/1916	18/09/1916
War Diary	W26D	19/09/1916	30/09/1916
Heading	War Diary A and Q Branches 23rd Division 1st October to 31st October Vol XIV		
War Diary	Camp W 26 D 3/4 Mili W. of albert adv HQ shelterwood	01/10/1916	02/10/1916
War Diary	Shelter Wood S of Contalmaison	03/10/1916	03/10/1916
War Diary	Shelter Wood	04/10/1916	08/10/1916
War Diary	Montigny	09/10/1916	11/10/1916
War Diary	Ailly Haut Clocher	12/10/1916	12/10/1916
War Diary	St. Riquier	13/10/1916	15/10/1916
War Diary	Busseboom	16/10/1916	19/10/1916
War Diary	Reninghelst	20/10/1916	31/10/1916
Heading	War Diary 23rd Division A and Q Branches 1st November 1916 to 30 November 1916 Vol XV		
War Diary	Reninghelst	01/11/1916	30/11/1916
Heading	War Diary 23rd Division A and Q Branches 1st December 1916 to 31st December 1916 Vol XVI		
War Diary	Reninghelst	01/12/1916	31/12/1916
Heading	War Diary 23rd Division A & Q Branches 1st January 1917 to Vol XVII		

War Diary	Reninghelst	01/01/1917	31/01/1917
Heading	War Diary 23 Division A & Q Branches 1st Feb 1917 to 28 Feb 1917 Vol XVIII		
War Diary	Reninghelst	01/01/1917	26/02/1917
War Diary	St Omer	27/02/1917	28/02/1917
Heading	War Diary 23 Division A & Q Branches 1st March 1917 to 31st March 1917 Volume XIX		
War Diary	St Omer	01/03/1917	19/03/1917
War Diary	Esquelbecq	20/03/1917	31/03/1917
Heading	War Diary 23rd Division A & Q Branches 1 April 1917 to 30 April 1917 Vol XX		
Miscellaneous	Connection during March 1917		
War Diary	Esquelbecq	01/04/1917	07/04/1917
War Diary	Busseboom	08/04/1917	30/04/1917
Heading	War Diary 23rd Division A & Q Branches 1 May 1917 Vol XXI		
War Diary	Bosseboom	01/04/1917	01/05/1917
War Diary	Winnezeele	02/05/1917	11/05/1917
War Diary	Busseboom	12/05/1917	31/05/1917
Heading	War Diary 23rd Division A & Q Branches June 1917		
War Diary	Bosseboom	01/06/1917	12/06/1917
War Diary	Berthen	13/06/1917	29/06/1917
War Diary	Zevecoten	30/06/1917	23/07/1917
War Diary	Merris	24/07/1917	24/07/1917
Heading	Adjutant Quarter Master General		

Woodstock 70/1 Gaugean

23RD DIVISION

'A' & 'Q' BRANCH.

AUG 1915 – ~~NOV 1916~~ 1917 JLY

DIARIES MISSING:-
~~MARCH & APR 1916~~
AUG, SEP, & OCT, 1917

To ITALY NOV. 1917

121/7595

H.Q. 23rd Divn. "A & Q"

Aug — Oct 1915

Vol. I

WAR DIARY
HEADQUARTERS
23rd. DIVISION.

A. A. & Q. M. G. BRANCH.

AUGUST 1915.

WAR DIARY
HEADQUARTERS
23rd. DIVISION.

A. A. & Q. M. G. BRANCH.

AUGUST 1915.

Army Form C. 2118.

WAR DIARY
INTELLIGENCE SUMMARY.
(Erase heading not required.)

Instructions regarding War Diaries and Intelligence Summaries are contained in F. S. Regs., Part II. and the Staff Manual respectively. Title pages will be prepared in manuscript.

Place	Date	Hour	Summary of Events and Information	Remarks and references to Appendices
BORDON	29/8/15	3 pm	Orders from A.T.C. for 23rd Division to proceed overseas. Advance party HAVRE 21st, Auto BOULOGNE 22nd — Divisions Entrains 23rd to E/F. G.S.O. 2 with party for HAVRE, + D.A.Q.M.G. with party for BOULOGNE. Orders issued warning all Officers + men from leave — detailing Advanced Parties, + preliminary details for the move. D.A. + Q.M.G. to remain at BORDON for the last Unit + the Surgeon is Ref[erence] Officer for Advanced Parties detailed on accordance with W.O. letter 10/1/27/57 Q.M.G.2 11/5/15. Wire to [?] Officer asking for balance of Field Motor Ambulance Establishment.	
BORDON	29/8/15		Orders from A.T.C. regarding details left behind. O.C. details at BORDON to be BRAMSHOTT apparently — Supernumerary 2nd Lieuts to act as Supernumerary Officers to the left behind details. Wire sent regarding T. Conveyances + Cavalry Maintd Transports Requisd. and corrected. Advanced party from HAVRE left for SOUTHAMPTON at 10 am by rail. Transport, cars & 16 other Officers arrived from GROVE PARK Transport Depot and were distributed.	
		10 pm	Motor Cars from BOULOGNE Advanced Party, left for FOLKESTONE with D.D.M.S. + D.A.D.M.S.	

Army Form C. 2118.

WAR DIARY
or
INTELLIGENCE SUMMARY.
(Erase heading not required.)

Instructions regarding War Diaries and Intelligence Summaries are contained in F. S. Regs., Part II. and the Staff Manual respectively. Title pages will be prepared in manuscript.

Place	Date	Hour	Summary of Events and Information	Remarks and references to Appendices
BORDON	22/8/15	8.30	Advance party from BOULOGNE left VIRTOD — the remainder of FOLKESTONE. On notification made delayed till four hours notice received.	
		2.30	Detailed Train from 23rd & 24th cancelled from N.T.O. and allotments to us cancelled. Failure to dispose of baggage & stores etc, surplus, received and distributed. Freight Movement	
BORDON	23/8/15	—	Asked N Times to complete move of Division to be distributed to all concerned. Fort Units of Division entrained BORDON SW at 5.35 p.m. After Base depot was safely detailed — Battery, Bakery etc Remainder party left FOLKESTONE for BOULOGNE at 10 p.m.	
BORDON	24/8/15	11 a.m.	Divisional Head Quarters Transport, Horses, Grooms, r.M.M.P. with A.P.M. & A.D.V.S. left BORDON for SOUTHAMPTON & HAVRE at 11 a.m.	

Army Form C. 2118.

WAR DIARY
or
INTELLIGENCE SUMMARY.
(Erase heading not required)

Place	Date	Hour	Summary of Events and Information	Remarks and references to Appendices
BORDON	25/8/15	3 pm	Divi. Headquarters less Advanced Parties & Transport Parties & Liphook Station. Divisional Headquarters left LIPHOOK for FOLKESTONE & BOULOGNE	
		5.55 pm	arrived at FOLKESTONE & Embarked for BOULOGNE	
FOLKESTONE		9.20 pm		
			Naval landed at BOULOGNE. D.A.P.M.G. by Embarkation Staff Officer as to accommodation arrived at BOULOGNE. Communicated orders received from G.O.C. R.A. General Staff. Camp Commandant.	
BOULOGNE	"	11.15 pm	Received & distributed Camp Commandant's accommodation details to Clerks & to Camp at OSTROHOVE billetted Officers & Hotel du LOUVRE G.O.C. and Staff Officers to report to D.A.Q.M.G. STONER who arranged by car 23rd Division to the billets in area ZUTKERQUE – EPERLECQUES & TILQUES	
BOULOGNE	26/8/15	9.30 a.m.	At DETESTMT Liaison Officer reported himself with car at Hotel Details from Camp OSTROHOVE proceeded to Railway Goods Yard G.O.C. & Staff Officers proceeded to billetting area by Motor Car	
TILQUES	26/8/15	11 a.m.	Arrived TILQUES at Chateau de HOQUET Staff at Chateau HOQUET General Staff reported to A.D.M.S. V.R.D. R.A. D.D.M.G., A.G.S.O.I, & Q.M.G. Reported to A.P.M. to A.A. & Q.M.G. & G.H.Q. Details Reconnaissance Car D.P., R.H.O. & D.D.T. D.D.S. reported also to P.P.M.G. Arrived G.H.Q. to Train S Accompanied to A.G. Officer the A.G. Branch also to staff of Army and Reported from the Division when G.O.C. & H.Q. Troops left. In the chief purposes & various Economy Officers informed the 23rd Division will also attach itself from Reserve of Divisions to the XI Corps Reserve Duration probably remain also for procure stay in present district forwarded to 10 days.	

WAR DIARY
INTELLIGENCE SUMMARY.

Army Form C. 2118.

Place	Date	Hour	Summary of Events and Information	Remarks and references to Appendices
TILQUES	27/8/15	—	Units coming in to the billeting Area. To G.H.Q. - saw D.D.S. and G.H.Q. Troops. Information regarding A.P.M's duties. Went round billets of 2 G.S. Staffords and Frame.	
TILQUES	28/8/15	—	Units arriving in the billeting area. To G.H.Q. with A.P.M. Visited H.Q. G.H.Q. Troops - also A.P.M. G.H.Q. to obtain information. D.A.A. & Q.M.G. (parted from BORDON) arrived by car.	
TILQUES	29/8/15	—	To G.H.Q. with D.A.A. & Q.M.G. went to the A.G. who explained carefully procedure re: Casualties returns generally - also to the Discipline Branch re: Courts Martial. To A.D.Q.M.G. General for rules re: infaresidence also to the Ammunition Branch. A.P.M.G. & D.A.A. & Q.M.G. of 11th Corps visited the Division. Report that refilling point needed supervision - owing to Corps Units arriving short of rations. The Supply Column had to make 2 trips to Rail Head.	
TILQUES	30/8/15	—	Report (informed) as regards unsatisfactory ordering of manuals. Visited Head Quarters 11th Corps with D.A.A. & Q.M.G. & Staff found there. Desired general harangue re: particularly returns to be enclosed. None required at present. Saw G.O.C. about securing Ration - reporting evidence of D.A.Q.M.G. etc. G.O.C. decided to apply for relief of D.A.Q.M.G. (Capt YOUNG)	

Army Form C. 2118.

(5)

WAR DIARY
~or~
INTELLIGENCE SUMMARY
(Erase heading not required.)

Instructions regarding War Diaries and Intelligence Summaries are contained in F. S. Regs., Part II. and the Staff Manual respectively. Title pages will be prepared in manuscript.

Place	Date	Hour	Summary of Events and Information	Remarks and references to Appendices
TILQUES	31/8/15	—	G.O.C. XIᵗʰ Corps expected, but he did not arrive. C.G.S. visited G.O. & G.I. Division. Reft. over Capt. Young, D.A.Q.M.G. forwarded to Headquarters XIᵗʰ Corps & the G.O.C. interviewed him. Report card to Capt. Young & was forwarded with copy. D.A.Q.M.G. XIᵗʰ Corps (Bt. Maj. R. FORD) visited G.O.C. & afterwards visited G.O.C. 68ᵗʰ & 70ᵗʰ Bdes. with the D.A. & Q.M.G. of the Division. Casualty Returns & Returns of Numbers Evacuated to Clearing Station Called for by XIᵗʰ Corps	

WAR DIARY
HEADQUARTERS
23rd. DIVISION.

A. A. & Q. M. G. BRANCH.

SEPTEMBER 1915.

Army Form C. 2118.

WAR DIARY
INTELLIGENCE SUMMARY.
(Erase heading not required)

Place	Date	Hour	Summary of Events and Information	Remarks and references to Appendices
TILQUES	31/8/15	—	G.O.C. XI Corps expected, but he did not arrive. C.G.S. visited G.O.C. of the Division. Report on Capt Young. D.A.Q.M.G. proceeded to Headquarters XI Corps. G.O.C. interviewed him – Permit card to Capt Young who was furnished with copy. D.A.D.M.S. XI Corps (B'd'd R. Ford) visited G.O.C. re 68th to 70th Brigades, also ADAH & DMS of the Division. Conference re MG of the Division. Casualty Returns, returns of numbers evacuated to Clearing Station called for by 11th Corps.	
TILQUES	1/9/15	—	Divisional Exercises – Head Quarters at SPERUECQUES – DAA & QMG attached to respect Q Branch of Staff. Casualty & Clearing Stations opened at 8.30 except RAMC Motor Ambee. Details of Casualty & Strength Returns received from 11th Corps, & carried to all concerned.	
TILQUES	2/9/15	—	Report to H.Q. of 11th Corps re Brig Genl Sir D. KINLOCH Com'd'g 70 Infy Bde – asking for him to be replaced by a younger Officer. List of Returns to be rendered. Pro Forma. Visited G.H.Q. rear AQMG personnel re report on Capt YOUNG D.A.Q.M.G. Numbers of vehicles for S.A.R. called for by 11th Corps.	

WAR DIARY
INTELLIGENCE SUMMARY

Army Form C. 2118.

Place	Date	Hour	Summary of Events and Information	Remarks and references to Appendices
TILQUES	3/9/15	—	Artillery Personnel arrived to complete the Ammunition Sub. Park. 6th Field Ambulance Report - Change of billet to La Communal. G.O.C. Guards Division (Lord Cavan) visited G.O.C.	
TILQUES	4/9/15	—	D.A.Q.M.G. (Gal. Taub) visited Divisions - went to Brit Train & saw O.C. Train. + Senior Supply Officer. O.C. 9 F.S. Supports reported case of impropriety in his Battalion - at orders of G.O.C. the A.D.M.S. saw 4 Officers + censured them. D.A.Q.M.G. Capt Young put in appeal to the G.O.C. Corps. Shall perform orders received from Division to move on 6th Sept to ARQUES – HAZEBROUCK Area. See Route fare 15th Army.	
TILQUES	5/9/15	—	D.A.Q.M.G. to 11th Corps to take orders as regards the move + billeting. He then proceeded to the billeting area, with the Staff Captains. Orders issued from the Staff billeting parties to meet the Staff Captains tomorrow. V.V. Cable Section ordered to Entrain with 11th Corps. The Supply Column + Ammunition Sub. Park proceed with us. D.A. + Q.M.G. 3rd Corps visited our Headquarters.	

Army Form C. 2118.

WAR DIARY
INTELLIGENCE SUMMARY.
(Erase heading not required.)

Place	Date	Hour	Summary of Events and Information	Remarks and references to Appendices
TILQUES	6/9/15	9 am	Headquarters Coy. "T" Coys. proceeded to CHATEAU de PRI-MAR- RENESCURES. Complaint from 11th Corps as to condition of Head Quarters buildings at RENESCURES. Saw D.A.+Q.M.G. 11th Corps on the subject.	
RENESCURE	6/9/15	11 AM	Headquarters established for the night. Long march for Troops: they found the pavé "sauté very trying + there was considerable straggling. Orders received that certain details of the 20th + 27th Divisions were to be attached to this Division, sent the Trenches for instruction. D.A.Q.M.G. + Staff Capt. Colonis proceeded to Mens billeting area - Orders issued to billeting parties.	
RENESCURE	7/9/15	9 am	Headquarters left RENESCURE & proceeded to MERRIS.	
MERRIS	7/9/15	11 AM	Headquarters established at MERRIS.	
			R.A. " " MERRIS.	
			Divre G.H.Q. " " MERRIS.	
			68. BDE " " MERRIS.	
			69 " " " LE VERRIER.	
			70 " " " OUTTERSTEENE.	
			A.D.M.S. + G.S.O.1. visited 20th + 27th Divisions & arrange details of attachment of units to this Division. Starting units to join 20th + 27th Divisions on 9th inst. Brought Pruneau + left today. Orders below refers to attachment of Units.	

Army Form C. 2118.

WAR DIARY
INTELLIGENCE SUMMARY.

Place	Date	Hour	Summary of Events and Information	Remarks and references to Appendices
MERRIS	8/9/15		D.A. & Q.M.G. & Chief Clerk visited H.Q. of 1st Cavy for instruction regarding returns &c. Capt HOWES Regtl Trainine, appointed DAQMG vice Capt YOUNG. List of returns required received from 3rd Corps.	
MERRIS.	9/9/15		Orders received from Capt YOUNG to report his engt. D.A & Q.M.G. 3rd Corps visited the Division.	
MERRIS	10/9/15		Visited 1st Ranrey Was-Separated reviewed "A" work with R.M.M.G. Seen the D.D.S & inspected new portable shelter for use of Cyclists. Capt HOWES joined & assumed duties of D.A.Q.M.G.	
MERRIS	11/9/15		Capt YOUNG, Late A.D.Q.M.G. & Lt-Col the Division. A.A. & Q.M.G & Dn.Q.M.G. visited the H.Q. of Division reappointed with the D.D.Q.M.G. visited Field Hospitals. Pte N. Bronnac, R.E. Signs Co. has been ordered to follow his Bn to Division. Bn Bugl Phillips 10th Ches. has to be Regtld in succession to R. Bugl Keiser Hulsoch.	

Army Form C. 2118.

WAR DIARY
or
INTELLIGENCE SUMMARY.
(Erase heading not required.)

Instructions regarding War Diaries and Intelligence Summaries are contained in F.S. Regs., Part II. and the Staff Manual respectively. Title pages will be prepared in manuscript.

Place	Date	Hour	Summary of Events and Information	Remarks and references to Appendices
MERRIS	12/9/15	—	Orders issued for the Relief of the Devonshires today for the following B'life. G.O.C. can 65th over for Exchange	
MERRIS.	13/9/15	—	Orders for move from Relief. D.A.M.G. & A.P.M. to go to Division to take of move Relief. Col. of Cog to 92nd Division. D.D.V.D.M.G. attached to Division.	
MERRIS	14/9/15	—	Visited 27th Division - Arrangements with D.D.O.M.G. related various points. 79th Brigade took over left sector of trenches.	
MERRIS	15/9/15	—	Arrangements for taking over have been received relieving fatigue parties. D.D. of A.G. H.Q. Army visited the Division.	
MERRIS.	16/9/15	8.30	Clerk leaves Divisional Head Quarters.	
CROIX DU BAC	"	9.A.M.	Took over. Dr H. Deyfrana 27th Division - G.O.C. took over 10 A.M. Verbal tour of regulation service to New area. G.O.C. started daily conference at 8.30.	
CROIX DU BAC.	17/9/15		Inspected area in the morning - Col. Guy 2nd a/g R.E. & D.M. Salvage Col. officer etc. Reported on Searching Area for Salvage fatigue parties.	

A.D.S.S./Forms/C. 2118.

WAR DIARY
INTELLIGENCE SUMMARY.
(Erase heading not required.)

Army Form C. 2118.

Place	Date	Hour	Summary of Events and Information	Remarks and references to Appendices
CROIX DU BAC.	18/9/15	—	C.R.E. 2nd Corps notified for Services. Visited the 3rd Corps & D.A. & released transport for R.E. work. 2nd Corps Sanitary Section. Salvage Coys — Sealed with G.O.C. & D.G.O.C.R.P. tied. heart telams. fair out Supply of Ammunition.	
CROIX DU BAC	19/9/15	—	Several Aeroplanes of both sides up, violently shelled. Conference regarding pending operations. D.A.Q.M.G. started Armourers Shop with details of 68th Brigade. 1 Company Pioneers to LA MOTTE for wood - Cutting fatigues. During the forthcoming Operations the whole of the Ammunition on the Sub-park is to be dumped at the D.A.C. in charge of an officer as an extra allowance. Horses & Records enclosed issued.	
CROIX DU BAC	20/9/15	—	Aeroplanes about the sky. Casualties by enemy shells dropping D.A.Q.M.G. visited Boat Camp & discussed questions of Trench Ammunition Grenades, Trench Mortars & Very Lights. B.D. & D.M.G. visited 8th Division & arranged that Casualties in R.A. Units attached to 8th Division be put on a parade states slowed to be reported by that Division. Chief Ordnance Officer manufacturing - arrived here to forward Reserve Grenades from C.O. Provision of Salvage Coy. Secretary Sup.Cy. to be from Charing XX Road in case of our Advance.	

Army Form C. 2118.

WAR DIARY
or
INTELLIGENCE SUMMARY.
(Erase heading not required.)

Instructions regarding War Diaries and Intelligence Summaries are contained in F. S. Regs., Part II. and the Staff Manual respectively. Title pages will be prepared in manuscript.

Place	Date	Hour	Summary of Events and Information	Remarks and references to Appendices
CROIX DU BAC	22/9/15	—	1st Army operations began being reported of a Larger General Scheme from the Heavy Expeditionary Force. 9th Division started Artillery bombardment about 9 a.m. 23rd ". 1 Section of 6th Reserve Park at STEENBECQUE, attached to this Division in place of General — D.A. & Q.M.G. 3rd Corps held discussed Tmsch Howitzer Ammunition Dep. C. & Schemes from pushing up Stores in case of emergencies.	
CROIX DU BAC	23/9/15	—	Bombardment of enemy's position continued — very little reply from Guns. Casualties. Inspected Cav. Divnl. Yard work proceeding satisfactorily.	
CROIX DU BAC	23/9/15	—	Rode out on programme of Roads & bonds in case of operations, in consultation with G.O.C. R.A. I.N.D.M.S. R.A.D. arranged system of stopping Posts etc with P.M. M.D.M.G. & D.M.D.M.G. 3rd Corps visited Division D.A. & Q.M.G. 1st Army came over to order a Ct-Martial on Lieut Flavey, same being in possession of a cornerade.	
CROIX DU BAC	24/9/15	—	Heavy Artillery fire being on all down the Line. Went to inspect the Carh. fatigues & Cound generally. G.O.C. & General Staff went out to advanced Headquarters. Stayed up practically all night dealing with reports.	

WAR DIARY
INTELLIGENCE SUMMARY.

Place	Date	Hour	Summary of Events and Information	Remarks and references to Appendices
CROIX DU BAC	25/9/15	—	Great attack began at 4 a.m. Visited Advanced Headquarters at 5.30 a.m. Handed joining orders on all ranks to him. Visited Railhead to see Supply Column and Officer i/c with personal horses. Saw the O.C. remounted with him. 100 German prisoners passed through Croix du Bac. Issued orders to Clearing the battlefield and disposing of material left behind. Visited Advanced Headquarters again at 6 p.m.	
CROIX DU BAC	26/9/15	—	68th Brigade ordered to join 20th Division — visited H.Qrs 20th Division to arrange details. Visited Advanced Headquarters.	
CROIX DU BAC	27/9/15	—	Owing to failure of attack by 84th Division, practically all the normal conditions were resumed. Fatigued parties commenced again. Advanced Headquarters returned to Croix du Bac. 68th Brigade returned from 20th Division.	
CROIX DU BAC	28/9/15	—	68th Brigade moved out again into the 20th Division area. They drew supplies at 23rd Division refilling Points. S.Q.M.S. Bates came into the Office as Chief Clerk i/p/Corens. Sergt Taylor returned to duty. Sergt. Evans & P¹e Lawton recommended for D.C.M.	

Army Form C. 2118.

WAR DIARY
INTELLIGENCE SUMMARY
(Erase heading not required.)

Instructions regarding War Diaries and Intelligence Summaries are contained in F. S. Regs., Part II. and the Staff Manual respectively. Title pages will be prepared in manuscript.

(13)

Place	Date	Hour	Summary of Events and Information	Remarks and references to Appendices
CROIX DU BAC	28/9/15	—	First Conference of Brigadiers & Heads of Departments held at 10 a.m. G.O.C. hour. R.A., A.D.O. + A.D. units leading to short replies which are to the issued to Monday in exchange for originals. D.M.T. + Cyclists handing in their bayonets. Orders issued for 10/- Crystal Pips toupet to be issued to unit. Visited Rat. H. Z. — Officer W.O. have a large amount of material.	
CROIX DU BAC	29/9/15	—	Conference 3rd Corps Advanced H.Dr.S. at 10 a.m. B.Gen G.S. presiding. D.M.Q.M.G. Now G.S.O.(1), A.D.M.G., V.C. R.E. F.B.O, 20 F., & 23rd Divisions present. Subject units hutting sessions. Relocate or Defences + Hutting to be equally divided. Paris Bullets to be taken in hand first. More accessories — bath & to be built. D.M.P. + D.M.G. + A.M.G. visited Advanced Hdqs. + 7th Bde H.D.S.S. also visited Baths + Salvage Company.	
CROIX DU BAC	1/10/15	—	A.M. + D.M.G. inspected Yeomanry Cold L Baths, M.P.H. + Salvage Company. Looked at "Homeless + Penniless". R.M. D.M.G. visited 3rd Corps + reviewed Conventional to Salvage Horrors + Pennants	
CROIX DU BAC	2/10/15	—	A.M., A.D.Q.M.G. + D.M.G. visit A.M.M. Armourer's Shop, + to & the Transport Depot. Exchanging long Rifles for short. P&C. R.M. A.M. visit to ARE Had God WTH = D.M.Q.M.G. 1st Army + Homeword + Penaes. Was also in exchange of Rifles. Preparing Schedules for Honors + Rewards.	

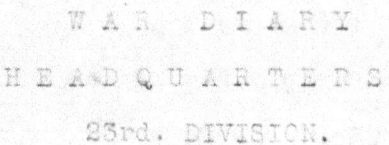

WAR DIARY
HEADQUARTERS
23rd. DIVISION.

A. A. & Q. M. G. BRANCH.

OCTOBER 1915.

WAR DIARY
HEADQUARTERS
23rd. DIVISION.

A. A. & Q. M. G. BRANCH.

OCTOBER 1915.

WAR DIARY
INTELLIGENCE SUMMARY

Army Form C. 2118.

Place	Date	Hour	Summary of Events and Information	Remarks and references to Appendices
Clock Bo Bae	1/10/15	—	P.M. + D.M.G. inspected Yeomanry, killed, Battn, A.P.M. Labaya Coy. Looked at Honours + Rewards. P.M. + D.M.B. Visited 3rd Coys & received armed forces to submit Honours + Rewards.	
Clock Bae	2/10/15	—	A.M. D.M.G. & D.A.D.M.G. visited A.P.M. Armourers Shop & 70 at Bala Thurpeer Shop. Inspecting Lang Rifles from Sheik — A.S.C. H.Q. R. ret landing; Shell Rifles. Visited A.M.E. Hdqrs D.D. + D.M.G. 1st Artillery Br Dela ~ 5/ of Rifles + Honours & Rewards. Prepared Schedule for Honours + Rewards.	

Army Form C. 2118.

WAR DIARY
INTELLIGENCE SUMMARY.
(Erase heading not required.)

Instructions regarding War Diaries and Intelligence Summaries are contained in F.S. Regs., Part II. and the Staff Manual respectively. Title pages will be prepared in manuscript.

Place	Date	Hour	Summary of Events and Information	Remarks and references to Appendices
Headqrs Croix du Bac	3/10/15		A.A. & Q.M.G. preparing the lists of Honours & Rewards	
Croix du Bac	4/10/15		Same as yesterday. D.A. & Q.M.G., 3rd Corps, verbal division sent to 3rd Corps & Reserved Honours & Rewards & handed in my list	
Croix du Bac	5/10/15		Nothing of importance to record.	
Croix du Bac	6/10/15		Weekly conference at 9 am. Cmdng. O.C. Trains, A.S.C. Officers & R.E. Officers appointed to Survey the Area & report on available Billets & requirements & accommodation.	
Croix du Bac	7/10/15		A.A. & Q.M.G. visited Refilling Point, Salvage Coy, Armourers Shop & Transport Depot. C.B.O. of Army visited the Division with reference to change of system beyond the movement with short rifles.	
Croix du Bac	8/10/15		A.A. & Q.M.G. and D.A.Q.M.G. visited Transport Camps	
Croix du Bac	9/10/15		A.A. & D.M.G. & D.A.D. M.G. visited the Train Camps - quite satisfactory. D.A. & Q.M.G. & 3rd Corps visited re Divisions	

WAR DIARY
INTELLIGENCE SUMMARY
(Erase heading not required.)

Army Form C. 2118

Instructions regarding War Diaries and Intelligence Summaries are contained in F.S. Regs., Part II. and the Staff Manual respectively. Title pages will be prepared in manuscript.

Place	Date	Hour	Summary of Events and Information	Remarks and references to Appendices
CROIX DU BAC	10/10/15	—	D.A. & Q.M.G. & D.N.Q.M.G. visited Ammunition Column — not very satisfactory. D.A. & Q.M.G. 3rd Corps visited the Division.	
CROIX DU BAC	11/10/15	—	D.A. & Q.M.G. 3rd Corps visited the Division. G.O.C. & D.A.Q.M.G. inspected billets in the afternoon. Orders received for 8 Vermorel Sprayers per unit chosen to 3rd Corps.	
CROIX DU BAC	12/10/15	—	Representatives of Graves Registration Commission (Lt Braithwaite) met Senior Chaplain & A.D.M.G. with reference to opening new cemetery at LA GUERMERIE. A case of G.A. & G. N.G. 3rd Corps visited the Division. G.O.C. & D.A.Q.M.G. inspected billets in the afternoon. Inspected by Lt Field Ambulance with A.D.M.S. with reference to those of G.S.	
CROIX DU BAC	13/10/15	—	Weekly conference at 9 a.m. lasted nearly 2 hours – points re-sully concerning General Staff. G.O.C. & D.O.C. Train inspected niece of the Battalion. Report in from Billetting Committee.	
CROIX DU BAC	14/10/15	—	D.Q.M.G. never received the billetting orders until O.C. Train & D.A.Q.M.G.	
CROIX DU BAC	15/10/15	—	70th Bde of 22nd Division ordered to billeting area with 22th Rd's & 21st Division. A.P. & Q.M.G. to H.Q. 8th Division to arrange details. D.A. & D.M.G. 3rd Corps motor'd round billets of D.A.C, Train, 40 V.L. & 12th Field. Transport with R.A. & D.M.G. & D.A.Q.M.G.	

Army Form C. 2118.

Instructions regarding War Diaries and Intelligence Summaries are contained in F. S. Regs., Part II. and the Staff Manual respectively. Title pages will be prepared in manuscript.

WAR DIARY
or
INTELLIGENCE SUMMARY.
(Erase heading not required.)

Place	Date	Hour	Summary of Events and Information	Remarks and references to Appendices
CROIX DU BAC	6/10/15	—	Staff Captain Int Bde visited Office to arrange details of interchange of Fatigues. DAQMG visited billets with OC Train.	
CROIX DU BAC	7/10/15	—	APMG visited billets with DAQMG & OC Train. Reported non receipt of returns from HQ RD. DAQMG visited HQ 8th Division re details of transfer. Bath rations & services. Shops receive visit from ADMG 8th Division.	
CROIX DU BAC	8/10/15	—	APMG 8th Division arrived the attached to this Office for a time. He visited the Divisional Baths, Mobile Baths, Mobile Fat. Camp. The Divisional Shops, Divisional Baths, & 70th Bde Mobile Fat. Camp.	
CROIX DU BAC	9/10/15	—	APMG 8th Division & DAQMG went round & co. trains & DMC. DAQMG 3rd Corps visited the Division. DAQMG visited the 2nd E. Lancs Regt at Fort Rompu.	
CROIX DU BAC	10/10/15	—	Weekly Conference — nothing of importance. Conference with CRE & OC Train regarding the Mutton Scheme. OC Train appointed to present the whole question. Principal Rules for drying Recruits vacuum buildings. No staff Conference in the evening.	
CROIX DU BAC	11/10/15	—	G.O.C. went round billets & horse lines with DMG. APMG & APQMG 8th Division visited 8th Division fusing factory & tomb spot. Staff Conference.	

2353 Wt W2544/1454 700,000 5/15 D.D.&L. A.D.S.S./Forms/C.2118.

Army Form C. 2118.

WAR DIARY
of
INTELLIGENCE SUMMARY.
(Erase heading not required.)

Instructions regarding War Diaries and Intelligence Summaries are contained in F. S. Regs., Part II. and the Staff Manual respectively. Title pages will be prepared in manuscript.

Place	Date	Hour	Summary of Events and Information	Remarks and references to Appendices
CROIX DU BAC	22/10/15	—	A.A + D.A.Q.M.G. visited JESUS FARM & the SALVAGE DEPOT. Ordered certain articles from latter place to be returned to the Divisions	
CROIX DU BAC	23/10/15	—	D.A.Q.M.G. visited hutts in the area. A.A.Q.M.G + D.A.Q.M.G visited billets at LA KOMANDERIE FARM. & inspected at the TOP camp of the 8th Stafford's - unsatisfactory and dirty	
CROIX DU BAC	24/10/15	—	A.A + D.Q.M.G. 3rd Corps visited the Divisions. Rotting stew of important	
CROIX DU BAC	25/10/15	—	A.A.Q.M.G. 8th Division returned to this Division D.A.Q.M.G. visited the billeting area.	
CROIX DU BAC	26/10/15	—	D.A + Q.M.G. visited the Divisions D.A.Q.M G. visited billets in the forward area. A.A + Q.M.G + D.A.A + Q.M.G. discuss the marketting arrangements in the Enquiry Line Road also the 68th Bde M-line Transport Camp. D.A.Q.M.G. to LA MOTTE to interview the Rail-Central Depot.	
CROIX DU BAC	27/10/15	—	Weekly conference at 7 p.m. nothing of importance. A.A + Q.M.G. visited D.A.Q + the Farsh farm which appeared to have been the & the latter was very good. A.A + Q.M.G + Baidoo Supply Officers met D.A.Q.M.G of 8th Corps, 1st + D.M.S, 18th Div. 9th Division at B.H.Q. ST MAUR. Battery - discussed possibilities of turning it into a double cord head Refilling point from the 2 Divisions	

Army Form C. 2118.

WAR DIARY
INTELLIGENCE SUMMARY.
(Erase heading not required.)

Instructions regarding War Diaries and Intelligence Summaries are contained in F. S. Regs., Part II. and the Staff Manual respectively. Title pages will be prepared in manuscript.

Place	Date	Hour	Summary of Events and Information	Remarks and references to Appendices
CROIX DU BAC	28/10/15	—	AA & QMG, DA & QMG, & SSO visited the Rifling Pacet Infantry billets at LA MONTAGNE and the firing & Camps of the 8th & 9th Yorkshire Regt	
CROIX DU BAC	29/10/15	—	DA.Q.M.G visited billets in the area. Nothing of importance	
CROIX DU BAC	30/10/15	—	AA&QMG) visited Right Sector of the Trenches with the D.A.Q.M.G & the A.D.C. Everything satisfactory. Enemy being quiet. D.A.Q.M.G went with G.O.C to visit the D.A.C. & some of the Battery Waggon Lines	
CROIX DU BAC	31/10/15	—	AA&QMG & O.C Trains visited ERQUINGHEM Billets, the R.E Park, the billets of the Survey Coy, the 14th Feild Amb. Headquarters R.F.A, Fd Amb, & 2 Battalions attached to 20th Division will billet shortly	

A.D. 23 ᵈ Sepᵣ: / Ansᵈ.
fol: 2

121/7635

Nov 15

Army Form C. 2118.

WAR DIARY
INTELLIGENCE SUMMARY.
(Erase heading not required.)

Place	Date	Hour	Summary of Events and Information	Remarks and references to Appendices
CROIX DU BAC	1/11/15	—	D.D.Q.M.G. visited area - arranged for perusal of Brigade depots & saw the unloading of coal returns by barge. A.D.Q.M.G. held first Administration Conference at 5.15 p.m. held weekly at this hour. Present D.D.Q.M.G, D.A.Q.M.G, D.A.D.O.S, D.A.D.V.S, A.D.M.S, P.M. Staff Captains, O.C. Trains, S.S.O, O.C. Sanitary Section & O.C. Salvage Coy.	
CROIX DU BAC	2/11/15	—	A.A & Q.M.G. visited 8th Division & interviewed A.A. & Q.M.G. on the subject of relieving an employed men. to the 21st Brigade completing Grenadiers, Signallers, Bandsmen, Divisional Fatigue Corps Employ, Tunnelling etc. also visited billets in the ERQUINGHEM ROAD. D.A.Q.M.G. and Comdr. visited the Division - ordered Baths to be procured. Lt. Col. Trevor reported himself & commenced Btn. K.O.Y.L.I.	
CROIX DU BAC	3/11/15	—	Weekly Conference. Subjects discussed - Hutting - Reserve of Smoke Helmets, Boot Shop - weight of land old. Decided to move the Divisional Boot Shop to ERQUINGHEM. Major Upton to HQ Office Estb. from D.A.Q.M.G. & Write on same.	
CROIX DU BAC	4/11/15	—	D.A.Q.M.G. left for England on Leave. D.A.D.O.S. Colonel visited the Division. Visited the 1st Line Transport Camp 69 Brigade, Bomb Depot & Erquinghem Camp. Leave duty in the G.S. Office.	
CROIX DU BAC	5/11/15	—	Major Upton carrying on duty in the morning. D.D.Q.M.G. interviewed the Filtering Area. Nothing else of importance happened.	

Army Form C. 2118.

WAR DIARY
or
INTELLIGENCE SUMMARY.
(Erase heading not required.)

Instructions regarding War Diaries and Intelligence Summaries are contained in F. S. Regs., Part II. and the Staff Manual respectively. Title pages will be prepared in manuscript.

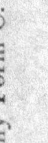

Place	Date	Hour	Summary of Events and Information	Remarks and references to Appendices
CROIX DU BAC	6/11/15	—	Major Upton went round to Billeting and Received orders to hand over 200 Mules to the MEERUT Division at 7 am D.A.C. at Nieppe. There was a very bad mistake on the part of the Meerut Division, who rang one from the Mules Office must telephoning, and said the Mules down to MERVILLE at 5.30 when they arrived there. The Remount Division had already taken over the Mules from the Division 4 am. Mules had come back.	
CROIX DU BAC	7/11/15	—	Report made to I.O. Corps about the Mules. Visited O.C. Train 24th Division at GOEDWERSWELDE. Very little of importance occurred.	
CROIX DU BAC	8/11/15	—	2nd in Command, Q.S. Eglandston came with complaint of dissatisfaction amongst officers - received him to put it in writing through his C.O. G.S.O.1 & A.P.M. & to a conference at 3rd Corps Headquarters re the reacttlement of Horses the Division & Co in 3rd Corps. Two Batteries & Co in Divisions (1 in Reserve the Division 1 Brigades (R/fg & R.A) and Battalions from Headquarters of Right Brigade of Left Division to move from ERQUINGHEM to LA ROLANDERIE.	
CROIX DU BAC	9/11/15	—	A.A. + Q.M.G., G.S.O. 3 + O.C. Trains to ROLANDERIE to inspect lands at Headquarters Motor billets in the vicinity. There are a piece suitable farms, but it was too far forward.	
CROIX DU BAC	10/11/15	—	Major Upton went for a round - billets of 1st Line Transport Corps Arranged with C.R.E. to commence work on LA ROLANDERIE.	

Army Form C. 2118.

WAR DIARY
of
INTELLIGENCE SUMMARY.
(Erase heading not required.)

Place	Date	Hour	Summary of Events and Information	Remarks and references to Appendices
CROIX DU BAC	11/9/15	—	A.A.+Q.M.G. & Major Lipton to the Infantry Recruits at L'HAZELDEAN. The wind was going on well. The C.R.E. makes new wet-ground with us on duty from the night to the office.	
CROIX DU BAC	12/9/15	—	D.A.Q.M.G. arrived from leave about 10. He had been delayed by the gales. Nothing for him occurred.	
CROIX DU BAC	13/9/15	—	D.A.Q.M.G. went round & inspected huts & horse lines - gave orders for the huts occ the PROVING REM. huts to be restored. Reports on the 69th Bde. Bomb School - instructor blew off bomb by mistake. 3 men killed + 16 wounded.	
CROIX DU BAC	14/9/15	—	D.A.Q.M.G. visited the Divisional Baths. Brig. Gen du BOURY visited the Division. La Gorgue general CHICHESTER's D.A.Q.M.G. 3rd Corps S. Inspected with C.R.E. selected site for huts for H.Qrs. Royal Brigade.	
CROIX DU BAC	15/9/15	—	A.A.+Q.M.G. D.A.Q.M.G. visited 68th & 69th Brigades Transport Camps. A.A.+Q.M.G. visited the Division - fixed the dividing line between the 2 areas with D.A.A.+Q.M.G. 3rd Corps + A.A.+Q.M.G. 8th Division. Weekly Administrative Conference in office A.A.+Q.M.G.	
CROIX DU BAC	16/9/15	—	D.A.+Q.M.G. 3rd Corps visited the Division. D.A.Q.M.G. went out round the area. D.A.A.+Q.M.G. went round to consult Employees re Chance sites for Regimental scores & People Store Rooms.	

Army Form C. 2118.

WAR DIARY
— or —
INTELLIGENCE SUMMARY.
(Erase heading not required.)

Instructions regarding War Diaries and Intelligence Summaries are contained in F.S. Regs., Part II. and the Staff Manual respectively. Title pages will be prepared in manuscript.

Place	Date	Hour	Summary of Events and Information	Remarks and references to Appendices
CROIX DU BAC	17/11/15	—	Weekly Conference 11 a.m. Resolutions re rations veto discussed. Loose allotment received no distributed to units. O.C. 92nd informed S.Staffords interviewed by G.O.C. who stated that this was not sufficient grounds to justify further action being taken.	
CROIX DU BAC	18/11/15	—	A.P. & D.M.G., Y.D.A.Q.M.G., visited T.O.D.A.G. & T.O. Train. The former appears were very unsatisfactory, & the latter were very good.	
CROIX DU BAC	19/11/15	—	3rd Corps Commander visited Divisional Baths. A.A.Q.M.G., D.A.Q.M.G., Y.A.D.M.S. accompanied the visit. He was satisfied with what he saw. Went on to Wittenmere from see but the Infantry. D.Q. MANSFIELD, 10th N. Robert Regt. attached to D.C. n. D.A.Q.M.G. 3rd Corps visited the Services. Arranged for Stables & Single keeping trains to be erected in the various billeting areas.	
CROIX DU BAC	20/11/15	—	Rationing & temperature improved. D.A.Q.M.G. visited ERQUINGHEM KILLS. ERQUINGHEM KILLS	
CROIX DU BAC	21/11/15	—	Proposed to start a Divisional School of Instruction at STEENWERCK. Lent Headquarters to the present Brence Regular Headquarters - Sent orderlies as guides billeting to O.C.D.M.T.	
CROIX DU BAC	22/11/15	—	D.A.Q.M.G. visited billets at ERQUINGHEM Ve Nieuxwig & ROUNDERIE in the afternoon arranged details of accommodation. Administration Conference - Battery preparations.	

2353 Wt. W2544/1454 700,000 5/15 D.D. & L. A.D.S.S./Forms/C. 2118.

Army Form C. 2118.

WAR DIARY

INTELLIGENCE SUMMARY.
(Erase heading not required.)

Instructions regarding War Diaries and Intelligence Summaries are contained in F. S. Regs., Part II. and the Staff Manual respectively. Title pages will be prepared in manuscript.

23

Place	Date	Hour	Summary of Events and Information	Remarks and references to Appendices
CROIX DU BAC	23/11/15	—	DA+ QMG visited the overseas Recreation Rooms & with G.O.C. 88th Brigade. DAQMG visited billets with the G.O.C. in the afternoon.	
Croix DU BAC	24/11/15		Weekly conference at 9 am. Conditions of horses discussed and arrangements for the accommodation of officers at the Divl School of Instruction. Claims officer reported supplies of gumboots arrived at 9.12. required for instruction in trench making would be available from 25th inst.	
CROIX DU BAC	25/11/15		DA+QMG attended a conference regarding new Divl Defence Scheme at 2.30. 16 head of ? reinforcements arrived.	
CROIX DU BAC	26/11/15		DAQMG visited Divisional Baths (new) HQ of 24th Infy Bde and Divl Ammn Column Coopers and horse lines. Improvement of Shelters at Jesus Farm begun by R.E.	
Croix DU BAC	27/11/15		An extra allotment of gum boots made for the units in the trenches.	
CROIX DU BAC	28/11/15		DA+QMG 3rd Corps visited the Division. DAA+QMG visited the 10 W. Riding Regt at Jesus Farm. DA+QMG visited the 6th & 69th Bde Transport Camps.	
CROIX DU BAC	29/11/15		DAA+QMG interviewed Qr Sgt Jn? L. Bde Ch ? Suby of Recreation Rooms.	
CROIX DU BAC	30/11/15		DQMG visited the Salvage Corps Refs? Bomb shop & the Divisional Baths. DAA+QMG visited Recreation Rooms.	
CROIX DU BAC	1/12/15		DAQMG visited Nº pickets? Divl Area to find billets for machine gun school. Weekly conference at 9am. Questions of horse rations, regulns for troops and washing of mens clothes discussed.	

2353 Wt W2544/1454 700,000 5/15 D. D. & L. A.D.S.S./Form/C. 2118.

Av.Ø. 23rd बिर.
Vol: 3

121/7936

SECRET

WAR DIARY

A & Q. BRANCH.

23rd DIVISION.

DECEMBER. 1915.

WAR DIARY

INTELLIGENCE SUMMARY.

Army Form C. 2118

Place	Date	Hour	Summary of Events and Information	Remarks and references to Appendices
CROIX DU BAC.	1/12/15	—	D.A.D.M.S. visited N practices of Divisional Area to find billets for Divis. Machine Gun School. Weekly Conference A.D.M.S. Practice of horse and foot vegetables for troops. Working party clothes issued.	
CROIX DU BAC	2/12/15	—	A.P. & Q.M.G. returned from leave. D.A.Q.M.G. visited the billeting areas & the Divisional Baths.	
CROIX DU BAC	3/12/15	—	D.A. & Q.M.G. Officer Short leave to England. D.A. & Q.M.G. 3rd Corps visited the baths area re laundering. Capt. LUNGFORD reported cases unsuited for duty via the office.	
CROIX DU BAC	4/12/15	—	Very bad weather — rain & wind. Starts with Y.M.C.A. advanced at BAC ST MAUR. Orders issued re Pioneer & Pier arrangements. Details of R.E. Guards & fatigue party A.P. & Q.M.G. visited Y.M.C. & Staff. 9th & 5th Staffords. Reconnaissance & Sand & Lone Officers on new billeting scheme — 2 days rail. Brigade to be in trenches.	
CROIX DU BAC	5/12/15	—	Showers — Nothing important occurred.	
CROIX DU BAC	6/12/15	—	Very bad weather — rain & wind. A.P.M. returned from leave. D.A. & Q.M.G. 3rd Corps visited the Divisions. D.A.Q.M.G. visited 50th Division re WERRIS to arrange billets re MINENWERFERS. O.C. 7th S. Staffs under interviewed re alleged neglect of duty by men R.M.C. Officer. A.G.M.S. 70th held administration Conference at 5.30 P.M.	

Army Form C. 2118.

WAR DIARY
~or~
INTELLIGENCE SUMMARY.
(Erase heading not required.)

Instructions regarding War Diaries and Intelligence Summaries are contained in F. S. Regs., Part II. and the Staff Manual respectively. Title pages will be prepared in manuscript.

Place	Date	Hour	Summary of Events and Information	Remarks and references to Appendices
CROIX DU BAC	7/12/15	—	Very bad weather – rain & wind. D.A.P.M.G. interviewed Staff Captain R.R. re hiring of Spanish grass for wagons.	
CROIX DU BAC	8/12/15	—	Weather fine & sunny. D.A.Q.M.G. visited to Divisional School in Morphine. Press retd. A.D.S. Conference – noted that A.A. wagons should stand on hard standings on fields.	
CROIX DU BAC	9/12/15	—	Very bad weather – wind & rain. The Germans shelled (SP) into Erquinghem for first time – little damage. Requested G.S.O.1 check back for no cause.	
CROIX DU BAC	10/12/15	—	A. L. visited – rain & storm. Of no interest. Germans shelled rear of Armentières Brewery & Ferme etc from about there from 9.30 a.m.	
CROIX DU BAC	11/12/15	—	Very unsettled – extremely heavy rain & high wind. Telephone communications killed. Brig'd out. P.C. telephone battery testing. Letter to Antrim Cinema cancelled to rest of div. Y.M.C.A. hut erected in 9 schools.	
CROIX DU BAC	12/12/15	—	Very bad weather, heavy rain & gale. American Expeditionary Ridge Batt. Joist Erquinghem Bridge nearly away. Ruft & Dressel 50 ta for minutes. Bombers visited cinemas & interesting part Rest of Bn. at 5a.m. in church. Orders yesterday no 3 & Needles Expected no 2 on hand	ref. issue form.

2353 Wt. W2344/1454 700,000 5/15 D. D. & L. A.D.S.S./Forms/C. 2118.

Army Form C.2.

WAR DIARY
or
INTELLIGENCE SUMMARY.
(Erase heading not required.)

Instructions regarding War Diaries and Intelligence Summaries are contained in F.S. Regs., Part II. and the Staff Manual respectively. Title pages will be prepared in manuscript.

Place	Date	Hour	Summary of Events and Information	Remarks and references to Appendices
CROIX DU BAC	13/12/15		Brigadier killed - funeral party. D.A. & Q.M.G. lectured to the Divisional Class at STEENWERCK on Courts Martial and Discipline.	
CROIX DU BAC	14/12/15		Weekly Conference at 9 a.m. At 11 a.m. Corps Commander presented ribbons to V.C. to Pte KENNY 13th Durham L. Infty - at RUE DORMOIRE. Battalion paraded & representations from all units in the Division. Posted & Generals of Cork GIBBORN, Bde Major R.A. at ERQUINGHEM at 3.30 pm A.P.M. 3rd Corps visited the office during afternoon about trial of a P.W.	
CROIX DU BAC	15/12/15		Confidential Reports on Staff in preparation. A.D.M.G. 3rd Corps visited Division - discussed questions of Hygiene Sanitation &c. D.D.O.S. 1st Army visited Division to arrange for ambulance stretchers	
CROIX DU BAC	16/12/15		Nothing to report	
CROIX DU BAC	17/12/15		D.A.A. & Q.M.G. visited the Recreation Rooms. D.A.Q.M.G. visited the Divisional Baths. Rate and list of reinforcements wanting requirements from K.C.R.E.	
CROIX DU BAC	18/12/15		Advance form Munition Workers to proceed to HAZEBROUCK. No cabs available in accordance with 3rd Corps Orders & visits therefore cannot at present take place.	

Army Form C. 2118

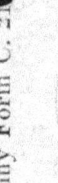

WAR DIARY
or
INTELLIGENCE SUMMARY.
(Erase heading not required.)

Instructions regarding War Diaries and Intelligence Summaries are contained in F. S. Regs., Part II and the Staff Manual respectively. Title pages will be prepared in manuscript.

Place	Date	Hour	Summary of Events and Information	Remarks and references to Appendices
CROIX DU BAC	19/12/15	—	D.A.Q.M.G. to STEENWERCK re billetting. Visited E.H.Q. suite Chinese Officers – Chinese at MOULLE SERIE.	
NOIX DU BAC	20/12/15	—	G.O.C. proceeded on leave. Brig. Gen. Carey B.C. to 7th Inf. Bde. assumed Command of the Division. D.A.Q.M.G. Bays Corps visited the Division. G.O.C. attended Schools for Commanders from D.L.O.Y. A.P.D. M.G. & G.S.O.W. visited Pierres of 11th Bulk Texas at L'HALLOBEAU.	
CROIX DU BAC	21/12/15	—	Nothing new. 2 Infantry & 2 R.A. officers out from England for reduction, 50 officers & 2/6 R.B. R.A. outers. 20 officers under orders G.O.C. R.N.	
CROIX DU BAC	22/12/15	—	G.O.Cs Conference a.m. AT A.P.D.M.G. meeting P.A.L.O. & D.A.Q.M.G. Inspect Divis Theatre & Recreation Room. A. Cap. of Permanent heating equipment forwarded to the C.R.E.	
CROIX DU BAC	23/12/15	—	D.P.Q.M.G. visited Depot. Refugee FLETCHER to leave at start he was given at BOIS GRENIER.	
CROIX DU BAC	24/12/15	—	Nothing to report.	
CROIX DU BAC	25/12/15	—	A.P.S D.Q.G. visited Xmas Dinners of Divisional Headquarters & G. "A" & "Q" Staffs.	
CROIX DU BAC	26/12/15	—	Nothing to report.	
CROIX DU BAC	27/12/15	—	Bad snow and thick Fog at dawn. D.A. & Q.M.G. visited Division re Inspect General Staff	

WAR DIARY
or
INTELLIGENCE SUMMARY.

Army Form C. 2118

Instructions regarding War Diaries and Intelligence Summaries are contained in F. S. Regs., Part II. and the Staff Manual respectively. Title pages will be prepared in manuscript.

Place	Date	Hour	Summary of Events and Information	Remarks and references to Appendices
CROIX DU BAC	28/9/15	—	G.O.C. returned from leave & re-assumed Command of 8th Division. D.A. & Q.M.G. visited Billets.	
CROIX DU BAC	29/9/15	—	D.A.Q.M.G. visited Billets. A.P.M. D.A. & Q.M.G. visited Y.M.C.A. hut who chief rented at A.P.M. Hdqt. D.R. Q.M.G. Battalion at STEENWERCK and NEUVE CHAPELLE.	
CROIX DU BAC	30/9/15	—	A.D.M.S., 3rd Brigade visited Division & inspected Reserve Bde. Billets & DORMOIRE, FORT ROMPU & LITTLE BEAU WELL. D.A. & Q.M.G. orders for medical arrangements for 8th & 9th Bde for attack Rctd.	
CROIX DU BAC	31/9/15	—	Sub Officer & 2 Unbarred Wagons & Advanced Remit. Stores for preparation for Attack. Grad. ambl. with Vermorel Sprayers served on 6th Rde reporting 1st Lot Soldiers not sufficient. Hot Wind strong wd. Soldiers transferred from D. Rde. Very bad accident at R.E. Store CHAPELLE D'ARMENTIÈRES. Att. possible blown to most of 3rd Bde Stores. Hy. all firing guns advanced supply Station used. Casualties about 30 killed, wounded including 10 Officers & 6 Labourers. Blown Supply Station.	

No.	Contents.	Date.
	23RD DIV. A. & Q. JULY-OCT. 1916 January to December 1916	

WAR DIARY
or
INTELLIGENCE SUMMARY.
(Erase heading not required.)

Army Form C. 2118.

Place	Date	Hour	Summary of Events and Information	Remarks and references to Appendices
2ANDIBAC	1/1/16	—	7.30 P.M. Two raids were made on the German trenches one right by 67th Bde (10th N Fus) near Loos by 67th Bde (9th N.F.) The raid by 10th Light infantry by overlight field scheme back – Bad see off the Enemy. Casualties 2 OR wounded. Second raid. Very Successful. Rec'd very slight casualties Rec'd very slight. D.A.Q.M.G. obtained 300 venue cigarettes for Xmas box for STEENWERCK conference as above.	
CBXDUBAC	2/1/16	—	D.A.A. + Q.M.G. attended one military & Civil court martial at STEENWERCK. During this young afternoon signals in trenches were all quiet.	
BACDUBAC	3/1/16	—	Report of visits and inspections of military brass & D.C. Ms received of B.Aug-of-Jany 1 B.S.O. 3 Artillery Brass & 6 B.C. etc. also Mem received. D.A.D.M.S. visited the Baths.	
CROIXDUBAC	4/1/16	—	D.H.Q.M.G. attended a conference at Corps Hdqrs regarding new British front line trenches.	
CROIXDUBAC	5/1/16	—	The chief pulled the Cd. 2 B.Bde / Bgdr Genl Wiera rendered Lectures of Cars as Carsias at 40 ROULERS of M army D.A.Q.M.G. found billets from the Anti-Routing Section. G.O.C. mobile or Genl at HQ & Army. Army Commander visited the Division	
CROIXDUBAC	6/1/16	—	D.Q.M.G. STEENWERCK to Billet HQ Anti. Routing Section. Received Mem to all classes. G.O.C. presented D.C.M. Ribbon to Sergt A Henn 6-Black Watch.	

2353 Wt. W3344/1454 700,000 5/15 D.D.&L. A.D.S.S./Forms/C.2118.

Army Form C. 2118.

WAR DIARY
of
INTELLIGENCE SUMMARY.
(Erase heading not required)

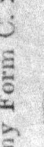

Instructions regarding War Diaries and Intelligence Summaries are contained in F.S. Regs., Part II and the Staff Manual respectively. Title pages will be prepared in manuscript.

Place	Date	Hour	Summary of Events and Information	Remarks and references to Appendices
CROIX DU BAC	7/1/16	—	G.O.C. presented D.C.M. ribbon to Pte Coluins. 8th Yorkshire Regt. A.D. & Q.M.G. 3rd Corps visited the Divisional Ironmongers and Supply Nenos & Correspondence.	
CROIX DU BAC	8/1/16	—	Wireless operators sent to Signal School. Received orders by mistake and carry out to Thur hut. Sept 2.00 Brecher bombs with Capt Bonner to 64 & Bde. Headquarters. Present the landing 2000 Brecher.	
CROIX DU BAC	9/1/16	—	A.A. & Q.M.G. visited the Refitting Point & the Y.M.C.A. hut. D.A.Q.M.G. to training at Steenwerck. Visited by the Bde H.Q.s with D.A.Q.M.G. an award of honour for MO's each.	
CROIX DU BAC	10/1/16	—	D.A.Q.M.G. lectured at STEENWERCK. 8th Colonels arrived from the high Command. A mine sent to each Brigade in the line.	
CROIX DU BAC	11/1/16	—	D.A.Q.M.G. lectured at STEENWERCK. 21st Division under a successful raid.	
CROIX DU BAC	12/1/16	—	G.O.C. weekly conference – a very short one. A.A. & Q.M.G. had a conference with Traffic Control, R.T. Train, A.D.M.S., R.E., D.A.D.O.S. & R.T.M. represented. D.A.& Q.M.G. 3rd Corps visited the Division. Wire to Smy. 3 officers selected to proceed to England for reconstitutions by H.M. The King, Pops Pancis D.A.Q.M.G. Cpl hills, R.T. Mops, Sergt Pike & Cpl Roberts Y. Worcesters.	

2353 Wt. W2544/1454 700,000 5/15. D.D. & L. A.D.S.S./Forms/C. 2118.

Army Form C. 2118.

WAR DIARY
or
INTELLIGENCE SUMMARY.
(Erase heading not required)

Instructions regarding War Diaries and Intelligence Summaries are contained in F.S. Regs., Part II. and the Staff Manual respectively. Title pages will be prepared in manuscript.

Place	Date	Hour	Summary of Events and Information	Remarks and references to Appendices
CROIX DU BAC.	13/1/16	—	Nothing special to record.	
CROIX DU BAC.	14/1/16	—	D.A.P.M.G. Offg. and Sturgis came to England on recce trip. Capt Knapp of A.S.C. to take acting D.A.Q.M.G. during recce. Major Faegre G.S.O. 3. to be O.H.E.R. to Staff Chapel Class.	
CROIX DU BAC.	15/1/16	—	A.D.M.G. had conference as to Traffic Control & presents the items in case. Colonel Knopf, Quick Master General, Staff Off. R.A. Maj. R.E., D.C. Train, S.S.O., D.A.D.O.S., D.A.D.M.S. A.P.M. Report compiled. Forward to Staff appd.	
CROIX DU BAC.	16/1/16	—	G.S.O.1 interviewed Major Lowndell & gave orders to Command 8th Yorks. Lt. Col. Thruston given orders of Reigning Command G.S. Staff. A.P.M. had 5 prisoners incarcerated in reading with civilians.	
CROIX DU BAC.	17/1/16	—	Cmr. O. visited 1st Division 2.30 am taken over 59th Infantry Brigade. Leave granted to Vincent J. Oliv Staff. Remarks post mortem. 15 Shells into ERQUINGHEM 8.30 pm.	
CROIX DU BAC.	18/1/16	—	Leave granted to Staff in connection for 5 days departure to Red. Rea. Red etc. Case will be recalled. Appreciation of Commanders from G.M.S. Staff. 8th Yorks with W. Yorks considered. A.P.M. G. & S.S.O. visited 20th Division in Red Rose & discussed details of work.	

Army Form C. 2118.

WAR DIARY
or
INTELLIGENCE SUMMARY.
(Erase heading not required.)

32

Place	Date	Hour	Summary of Events and Information	Remarks and references to Appendices
CROIX DU BAC	19/1/16	—	G.S.O.2. went on leave. G.O.C's weekly conference 9 p.m. short one.	
CROIX DU BAC	20/1/16	—	Heard that 20th Division were to relieve 34 Division prior to that Division going to Festuberk area from 34 Corps. O front of 4th Division, 28 Battalions of 1 Field Coy & one Fd Ambulance per Regt. Conference of Staff Captains relating to attachment of 34 Divisions Units.	
CROIX DU BAC	21/1/16	—	G.O.C. interviewed Lt Col Thwaites for S.Staff vacant have been pending resignation. Preliminary arrangements made for attachment until after 20th By's 622 By's artillery returned from leave.	
CROIX DU BAC	22/1/16	—		
CROIX DU BAC	23/1/16	—	O.C. Train 34th Div'n. came over to confer regarding supply arrangements received later by Dictation from 34th Div'n 6. 23rd Div'n. O.C. Train & Sen Supply Officer 23rd D present. RA's OC proceeded on 8 days leave.	
CROIX DU BAC	24/1/16	—	The A.A. & Q.M.G. 34th Div'n. came over to confer regarding the arrangements for the attachment of units of 34th Div'n to 6. 23rd Div'n for instructions. The Staff Captains of 1st Inf Bde reported here in the morning for instructions regarding the billeting of 15 and 15th (?) R. Scots belonging to 24th Bde. HQ 10/Royal Inde. 207 adj. Cpl RE 14a 10/Rgn Bde 20 Telop PET	
CROIX DU BAC	26/1/16	—	Weekly conference at 9 pm 15 & 16 R. Scots arrived here for attachment. 2 Bn when instruction. Conference at from Mn.A OC Trains & 3D re future supply arrangements	
CROIX DU BAC	27/1/16	—	DAA+QMG went to 3rd Corps H.Q. to interview the DA+QMG regarding Rations to horses & arrangements for supplies during the attachment of 34th Div's. DAQMG visited HQ 101 1st Bde	

2353 Wt. W2344/1454 700,000 5/15 D.D.&L. A.D.S.S./Forms/C. 2118.

WAR DIARY or INTELLIGENCE SUMMARY

Army Form C. 2118

Place	Date	Hour	Summary of Events and Information	Remarks and references to Appendices
CROIX DU BAC	28.1.16		O.C. 34th Div. Train came over to make arrangements for supplies in connection with move of H.Q. + 2 battns. of 101st Bde on Feb 1st.	
	29.1.16			
	30.1.16			
	31.1.16		AA & QMG 34th Division came over to be attached to the Division and A.Q. + Army went over to the 34th Division in his place.	
	1.2.16		13a & 16th R.S. (34th Division) relieved by 10th Lincoln + 11th Suffolk in ? Dugout Head Quarters remain attached. A.Q. Army (34th Div) visited Bn. H. Qrs. Station Railway Pmt and Baths at St Croix + 23rd Division MLO Lazarvetuin + Bat. Shops W. 02 Brigade. Weekly expenses at 9 pm. The question of the Transport of the train N & Q 2nd Bn. keeps up the ...	
	2.2.16			
	3." "		Visit by an army 34th Bn. of Canopu in ... area	
	4." "			
	5.2.16		A.Q. Army 34th went to Blaringhem with officers to see	
	6.2.16		A.Q. Army 14th visited 2nd his forks. Anonna Pat. Amifranai Pom in morning. taken in afternoon. Works aux the front line	
	7.2.16		away. Visited. Bombing School.	
	8.2.16		A.Q. Army 23rd Bn. J.O.C. Train 34th Brit. came over to discuss supply question. also consulted with the Com of the 2 Divisions	
	9.2.16		A.Q. Army 3rd & 4th North ... to H.Qs 30th Div in connection with 30th Div. move into forward area	

"A.V.Q." 23 w. D.W.
vol 5

Army Form C. 2118.

(34)

WAR DIARY
or
INTELLIGENCE SUMMARY.
(Erase heading not required.)

Instructions regarding War Diaries and Intelligence Summaries are contained in F. S. Regs., Part II. and the Staff Manual respectively. Title pages will be prepared in manuscript.

Place	Date	Hour	Summary of Events and Information	Remarks and references to Appendices.
CROIX DU BAC	10/2/16	—	A.P. + Q.M.Gs 23rd + 34 Divisions returned to us now Divisions	
CROIX DU BAC	11/2/16	—	EQUIPMENT shelled by the Germans Y BAC ST MAUR.	
CROIX DU BAC	12/2/16	—	DA + Q.M.G. + O.C. Train inspected lorries in the forenoon. Afternoon A.A.Q.M.G. attended Conference at Corps Headquarters - Subject: Hay etc. Chief orders etc. D.A.D. + Q.M.G. inspected Echelon Regade lorries A.P. + Q.M.G. represented by Bde. Tn. Comdrs.	
CROIX DU BAC	13/2/16	—	A.D.M.G. inspected 51st + 68th Reigt Tricycle Corps - Lateral etc. D.A.D.M.G. inspected Reserve Fougolla Recce.	
CROIX DU BAC	14/2/16	—	Very busy day carrying final details of Scheme of 69 + Brigade. D.A.D.M.G. passed Division rehearsed the march of Brigade in case Refund was again the Bde. A.P. + Q.M.G. + D.Q.M.G. visited R + A DERIE H.Qs + Reserve at Q. EQUIPMENT gave instructions as regards of Scheme.	
CROIX DU BAC	15/2/16	—	D.A.Q.M.G. visited Sector as regards hutting. Raid amount of Straw has been put (again) in of packing. D.D.U.S. arrived + inspected RPRO + Bee Hut. About to Concussion. He spread hospital D.A.Q.M.G. inspected stables.	

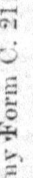

Army Form C. 2118.

WAR DIARY
INTELLIGENCE SUMMARY.
(Erase heading not required.)

Instructions regarding War Diaries and Intelligence Summaries are contained in F. S. Regs., Part II. and the Staff Manual respectively. Title pages will be prepared in manuscript.

(35)

Place	Date	Hour	Summary of Events and Information	Remarks and references to Appendices
CROIX DU BAC	16/2/16	—	Very heavy gale - did considerable damage. D.A. & Q.M.G. with D.D.A. & Q.M.G. 34th Divn. inspected 65th Rly Tpt Camp. 4th Corps T. St Omer. Visited billets in the RUE DELETTREE with a view to their improvement. G.O.C. weekly Conference at 6 p.m.	
CROIX DU BAC	17/2/16	—	D.A.Q.M.G. sick. D.D.A. & Q.M.G. Conference of G.H.Q. on Experience of Divisions. A.A. and Q.M.G. with C.R.E. visited billets at RUE DELETREE made some arrangements for its improvement. G.O.C. declared apply, shown A.A. & Q.M.G. relieved of his appointment.	
CROIX DU BAC	18/2/16	—	D.A. & Q.M.G. still sick. D.A. & D.Q.M.G. visited Rest Stations D.A. & D.Q.M.G. visited billets on the Reserve area. D.D.Q.M.G. still sick. Brig. commanding Division & 2nd Brigade &c.	
CROIX DU BAC	19/2/16	—	D.A.Q.M.G. sick. D.A.P. & Q.M.G. visited billets at JESUS FARM & HALLOBEAU. Conference of Transport Officers in A.A. & Q.M.G.'s Office.	
CROIX DU BAC	20/2/16	—	Actg. Q.M.G. & MME. BARRY's to negotiate for Hospital accommodation for field D.D.Q.M.G. still sick.	
CROIX DU BAC	21/2/16	—	A.A. & Q.M.G., D.A. & Q.M.G. Bat. Comps. D.D.M.S. 3rd Corps. met at MME. BARRY's. Reportstead agreed to & premises requisitioned by A.A. Q.M.G. in chief ordered from 3rd Corps. Period not requisition shown to signed by Corps Commander.	

2353 Wt. W2544/1454 700,000 5/15 D. D. & L. A.D.S.S./Forms/C. 2118.

WAR DIARY
or
INTELLIGENCE SUMMARY.

(Erase heading not required.)

Army Form C. 2118.

Place	Date	Hour	Summary of Events and Information	Remarks and references to Appendices
CROIX DU BAC	22/7/16	—	Orders to proceed to ESTAIRES and not into Rest Recommenced. Troops stopped pending further orders. Pulled changed to LA GORGUE owing to shelling of BAC ST MAUR. Rifle Park changed to STEENWERCK - TROIS ARBRES Road.	
CROIX DU BAC	23/7/16	—	D.A. & Q.M.G. 34th Division arrived to take over the office. Reinforcements received – ESTAIRES. Conference at H.Qrs 34 Division – A.A. & Q.M.G. 25 & 23rd Divisions, 1 D.A. & Q.M.G. 3rd Corps. Future movement & areas discussed.	
CROIX DU BAC & ESTAIRES	24/7/16	—	Handed over left area to 34 Division at 11 am and transferred Headquarters to ESTAIRES. Fresh accounts of the above. Nothing definite settled about the troops area. Busy making arrangement for troops.	
ESTAIRES	25/7/16	—	Very busy day settling down various arrangements for present position of future developments. Orders received late to go to the Rest Area for all B.A. & Q.M.G. 3rd Corps visited the Division.	
ESTAIRES & BLARINGHEM	26/7/16	—	Headquarters transferred to the Rest Area. Lect'ed D.A.A. & Q.M.G. A.M. & Q.M.G. & D.A. & Q.M.G. visited the 3rd Corps for areas.	
BLARINGHEM	27/7/16	—	Busy settling down in new area. Movement & Remounts conferences. Received two precaution telegrams. Deal found area with the A.D.M.S. trying to find a site for Special 10th hospital without result. D.A. Q.M.G. visits the Divisions are ordered. A.A. & Q.M.G. receive instructions to proceed to TOUCHET to take over from 61st Division. A/Major D. Standard. G.S.O.(1) & A.A. & Q.M.G. to 1st Army.	

Army Form C. 2118.

WAR DIARY
— or —
INTELLIGENCE SUMMARY.
(Erase heading not required.)

Instructions regarding War Diaries and Intelligence Summaries are contained in F. S. Regs., Part II. and the Staff Manual respectively. Title pages will be prepared in manuscript.

Place	Date	Hour	Summary of Events and Information	Remarks and references to Appendices
BETHUNE HEAD	28/2/16	—	Head Quar Sal-uc. Reported accproced buses received with the Felicitation to order from the Reva. Came 530 8 piece - oats + Twenty of midnight samosas How made getting ready the Horses + Limbers. G.O.C gave up his last hop the Dog cats. Orderlies received from Shd Corps about 8. Very busy making arrangements for there.	
BLARING HEM & BRUAY	29/2/16	—	DADQMG went there more to billets at 7 AM. DAAQMG 6 STEENBECQUE Transferred Headquarters of BRIAY at 11 am. Broke down about 2 p.m. AA + QMG JDM rems AA + QMG visited billets + received reports in connection with the road rates. Such arrangements for Refilling + Supply generally.	

Army Form C. 2118.

WAR DIARY
or
INTELLIGENCE SUMMARY.
(Erase heading not required.)

Instructions regarding War Diaries and Intelligence Summaries are contained in F. S. Regs., Part II. and the Staff Manual respectively. Title pages will be prepared in manuscript.

Place	Date	Hour	Summary of Events and Information	Remarks and references to Appendices

A & Q
23rd Div
Vol 6

Army Form C. 2118.

WAR DIARY
INTELLIGENCE SUMMARY.
(Erase heading not required.)

Instructions regarding War Diaries and Intelligence Summaries are contained in F.S. Regs., Part II. and the Staff Manual respectively. Title pages will be prepared in manuscript.

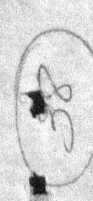

Place	Date	Hour	Summary of Events and Information	Remarks and references to Appendices
BRUAY	1/3/16	—	D.A.Q.M.G. visited all the Units & inspected Billets. D.A.A. & Q.M.G. went to CAYEUX RICHOURT Station & Superintended removal of baggage. A.P. to U.G. visited R.E. & A.S.C. Regts. on subject of Horses & Records. Divisions are now Rations & replenished with Reserves.	
BRUAY	2/3/16	—	Handed over billeting to D.A. & Q.M.G. New Pier. Billets Reinforced — D.A.Q.M.G. went round & visited it. & to erected units & to. A.A. M.G. working on Horses & Records all day. Got mostly thru finished Orders received for Major H.B. de V. WILKINSON to relieve Lt Col BYRNE as D.A.Q.M.G. of this Division.	
BRUAY	3/3/16	—	A.A. & Q.M.G. went out billeting — D.A.Q.M.G. visited Billeting parents late. A.A. & Q.M.G. worked at Horseurs Test. Orders came in as regards Relief. Conference with G.S. as regards Billeting & Village Areas allotted temporarily.	
BRUAY	4/3/16	—	G.O.C. had conference at 9 am. Settled the movement allowances so far as they are known. A.A. & Q.M.G. Billeting O.W. Q.M.B. visited 4th Corps to arrange Ordnance, Transport & Supply details.	

WAR DIARY
or
INTELLIGENCE SUMMARY
(Erase heading not required.)

Army Form C. 2118.

38

Place	Date	Hour	Summary of Events and Information	Remarks and references to Appendices
BRUAY	1/3/16	—	D.A.Q.M.G. visited all the Units Formations & inspected Billets. D.A. & Q.M.G. went to CHOQUE & BRUAY Stations & superintended removal of baggage. A.D.S.T. visited R.E. & 82nd Brigade on subject of Brooms & Firewood. Divisions alb 1000 Rations & replenished with Reserves.	
BRUAY	2/3/16	—	Handed over billetting to D.A.A.& Q.M.G. & went out to inspect & report upon the Supa Brigade Refilling Point & returned. — D.A.Q.M.G. went round & visited all new billets. A.A. & Q.M.G. working on Honours & Rewards all day got most of them finished. Orders received that Major H.B. McV. WILKINSON to relieve Lt Col BURNE as D.A.Q.M.G. of this Division	
BRUAY	3/3/16	—	A.A. & Q.M.G. went out billetting. — D.A.Q.M.G. visited Refilling points &c. A.A. & Q.M.G. worked at Honours list. Orders came in as regards Sabots. Conference with G.S. as regards billetting & villages values allotted Temporarily.	
BRUAY	4/3/16	—	G.O.C. had Conference at 9 am. Settled the Numbers Horses released so far as they are known. A.A. & Q.M.G. billetting D.Q.M.G. visited villages to arrange Billets &c. Transport & Supply details.	

WAR DIARY
or
INTELLIGENCE SUMMARY.
(Erase heading not required.)

Army Form C. 2118.

Place	Date	Hour	Summary of Events and Information	Remarks and references to Appendices
BRUAY	April		Nothing to report	
	5/3/15		1st, 2nd Bde & 13th & 69th Bdes move up to G¹², P², and GOUY Servins also a portion of 128th M RE	
"	6/3/15		A few infantry move to NOTRE DAME LORETTE and left sector of trenches respectively. Remainder of 69th Inf Bde move up to the 3 SERVINS	
"	7/3/15		2nd Inf Bde (less 1 Bn.) moving to the 3 SERVINS - 101st & 102nd & 76th M RE move up to ABLAIN ST NAZAIRE Remainder of 69th Bde move up to trenches.	
Ch de la HAIE	8/3/-		Remainder of division move into the area - Divisional head Quarters established by 1st Col LAMBERT at Chateau of la HAIE	
"	9/3/15		B. Gen DERHAM succeeded by Lt Col LAMBERT 2 i/c Lancs in command of 69th Inf Bde	
	10/3/15		24th Brigade relieves 69th Brigade in trenches - Railhead to HERSIN	

Army Form C. 2118.

WAR DIARY
or
INTELLIGENCE SUMMARY.
(Erase heading not required.)

Instructions regarding War Diaries and Intelligence Summaries are contained in F. S. Regs., Part II. and the Staff Manual respectively. Title pages will be prepared in manuscript.

Place	Date	Hour	Summary of Events and Information	Remarks and references to Appendices
BRUAY	[illeg]		Nothing to report	
	5/3/15		1st, 2nd R.de, 1.13" & 69th B.de move up to G.H.Q, P.C, and GOUY also a portion of 128" C. of R.E	
"	6/3/15		A few infantry move to NOTRE DAME LORETTE and left sector of trenches respectively. Remainder of 69th Inf. B.de move up to the 3 SERVINS	
"	7/3/15		2.4" Inf. B.de move up to the 3 SERVINS - (less 1 Btn.) 101st & 102nd F.C. of R.E move up to ABLAIN ST NAZAIRE. Remainder of 69th B.de move up to trenches.	
Ch. de la HAYE	8/3/15		Remainder of division move into the area - Divisional Head Quarters established in Chateau de la HAYE	
"	9/4/15		B. Gen DERHAM succeeded by Lt Col LAMBERT 2/E. Lancs in command of 69th Inf. B.de	
	10/3/15		2.4" Brigade relieves 69th Brigade in trenches. Head Quarters to HERSIN	

Army Form C. 2118.

WAR DIARY
or
INTELLIGENCE SUMMARY.
(Erase heading not required.)

Instructions regarding War Diaries and Intelligence Summaries are contained in F.S. Regs., Part II. and the Staff Manual respectively. Title pages will be prepared in manuscript.

Place	Date	Hour	Summary of Events and Information	Remarks and references to Appendices
CHATEAU de la HAIE	11/3/16		Tunnelling company moved from mines in the division	
			Honours Rewards and anything sent to III Corps. Orders received for move to 2nd Divisional area to the North. Corps school at PERNES for instructing men in various classes opened.	
	12.3		Orders received for move of the Division to 47th Division area near BRUAY and thence with the 2nd Division area near Herdin.	
	13.3		23rd Division commenced to move out of area and 47th Division move in in relief.	
	14.3		Relief of division continued. Reserve Group 23rd Divisional Engineers relief of 2nd Gp. D. Art. Res. Reserve Group 23rd Div RA completed relief " " " S.S. Officers relief Pioneers of 2nd Division. RE commence relief of RE of 2nd Division.	
	15.3		Relief of 2nd and 47th Divisions completed.	

2353 W. W2544/1454 700,000 5/15 D.D.&L. A.D.S.S./Forms/C. 2118.

Army Form C. 2118.

WAR DIARY
or
INTELLIGENCE SUMMARY.
(Erase heading not required.)

Instructions regarding War Diaries and Intelligence Summaries are contained in F.S. Regs., Part II. and the Staff Manual respectively. Title pages will be prepared in manuscript.

Place	Date	Hour	Summary of Events and Information	Remarks and references to Appendices
CHATEAU de La JAIE	11/3/16		Tunnelling Company formed from miners in the division. Honours Rewards and mentions sent to III Corps. Orders received for move to 2nd Division area to the North. Corps school at PERNES for instructing men in various classes opened.	
	12.3		Orders received for move of the Division to 47" Div" area near BRUAY and there into the 2nd Div area near Houdain.	
	13.3		23rd Division commences to move out of area and 47" Division move in in relief.	
	14.3		Relief of division continued. Reserve group 23rd Division Recommences relief of 2nd Div. Art Bde.	
	15.3		Reserve group 23" Div RA completes relief. S Staffords relieve Pioneers of 2nd Division. RE commence relief of RE of 2nd Division.	

Army Form C. 2118.

WAR DIARY
or
INTELLIGENCE SUMMARY.
(Erase heading not required.)

Instructions regarding War Diaries and Intelligence Summaries are contained in F. S. Regs., Part II and the Staff Manual respectively. Title pages will be prepared in manuscript.

Place	Date	Hour	Summary of Events and Information	Remarks and references to Appendices
BRUAY	16/8/15		Division HQ moves to BRUAY in relief of HQ 3rd N.R.	
			2/4th Bde moves to DIVION area	
			68th 13th " " COUPIGNY "	
			69th 13th " in BRUAY area	
			R.A. in 47th Div area less one Bde in 2nd Div area	50
	17/3		Further dispositions within Divison of 23rd Division from BRUAY area in to 2nd Division area	40
			(HERSIN - AIX NOULETTE) begins	
	18/3		R.A. commences to move back to rejoin units in relief of 47 Div R.A.	
			Their role as 2nd Div arm continued.	
			Arrangements made for a stop for 8th Div and unloading at HERSIN	40
	19/3		Move of 8th Division continues	20
			Active enemy middle fire showing observe on the	
	20/3		Moves continues	30
	21/3		68th Bde established in CALONNIE sector	
			69th " " ANGRES "	
			" " SOUCHEZ sector	
			9 Officers from England attached to the Division for short course of instruction	

Army Form C. 2118.

WAR DIARY
or
INTELLIGENCE SUMMARY.
(Erase heading not required.)

Instructions regarding War Diaries and Intelligence Summaries are contained in F. S. Regs., Part II. and the Staff Manual respectively. Title pages will be prepared in manuscript.

Place	Date	Hour	Summary of Events and Information	Remarks and references to Appendices
BRUAY	18/3/17		Divisional H Q move to BRUAY in relief of 47" Div. H.Q.	
			2nd Bde move to DIVION area	
			68 - 13th - " - COUPIGNY -	
			69 - 13th in BRUAY area	
			R.A. in 47" Div. area. Gas one B.de in 1st Bd area		AO
			Foldes Kinsfeld areas	
		11/3	move of 13rd Division from BRUAY area in to 2nd Division area	AO
			(HERSIN - AIX NOULETTE) begins	
		18/3	R.A. commence to move back to home area in relief of 47" Div R A	
			Inner wert 2nd Div area continued	
			Arrangements made for a show to collect and unloading at HERSIN	AO
		19/3	move of the division continues	
			Arrangement made for drawing stores baths	AO
		20/3	Process continues	AO
			63rd Bde established in CALONNE area	
			69 - " - ANGRES "	
		21/3	- " - SOUCHEZ action	
			9 Officers from England attached to the Divisions for short courses of instruction	AO

Army Form C. 2118.

WAR DIARY
or
INTELLIGENCE SUMMARY.
(Erase heading not required.)

Instructions regarding War Diaries and Intelligence Summaries are contained in F. S. Regs., Part II. and the Staff Manual respectively. Title pages will be prepared in manuscript.

Place	Date	Hour	Summary of Events and Information	Remarks and references to Appendices
SAINS en GOHELLE	22/3		2nd and 3rd went to SAINS EN GOHELLE	MO
	23/3		A.A. 23 are commencing repair of 2 new huts from Country engineers. R.A. works continues. MO Ant had moved to BARLIN expecting attack and supply wagons MO	
	24/3		R.A. relief completed. MO Early morning strafe Sainhain is now out of artillery	
	25/3		Temporary boundary started at HERSIN B-OP. working at 3 Telegraph Battery Loos Sector. MO Reagates Somme started at POSTS 10 and GOHELLE	MO
	26/3		No change	MO
	27/3		Our O.P. S. Staffords moved up to NOULETTE wood	MO
	28/3		M.O. change. 450 Boche from BARLIN villages arrive for carrying	
	29/3		John Robinson wd. Cpl S.J. and 2cl. Bryants 402 General Smith Inspection at 6.30 p.m.	
	30/3		Harms newspr demonstration at the bomb school 300 Country around is working party for signals. 5th Inf Bde address 99th Inf Bde 2nd Div no reserve Brigade.	Hollywood "11" A.H.R. P.11.9 2.3
	31/3		No change	MO

2353 Wt. W23H/1454 700,000 5/15 D. D. & L. A.D.S.S./Forms/C. 2118.

WAR DIARY
or
INTELLIGENCE SUMMARY.

(Erase heading not required.)

Army Form C. 2118.

Instructions regarding War Diaries and Intelligence Summaries are contained in F.S. Regs., Part II. and the Staff Manual respectively. Title pages will be prepared in manuscript.

Place	Date	Hour	Summary of Events and Information	Remarks and references to Appendices
SAINS EN GOHELLE	21/3		Bde H.Q. move to SAINS EN GOHELLE	HS
	22/3		RA 23rd Bde commences relief of 2nd Bn RA at 6.30 pm. Several weekly conference. RA never move to BARLIN refilling direct onto supply wagons in. Reached moved to BARLIN refilling direct onto supply wagons in	HS
	24/3		RA relief completed. Daily conference start situation & an attack of infantry	HS
	25/3		Temporary laundry started at HERSIN. Baths nothing at 3 places and 2 clothing Battalions Hersabir men started at POISO 10 and GOHELLE	HS
	26/3		No change	HS
	27/3		One Coy 1st S.S. supports moved up to ANOULETTE wood	HS
	28/3		No Change Battn from DRURY attacking wires for training	HS
	29/3		Inter Battalion relief on 65th and 2nd Brigades Several weekly conference at 6.30 pm	HS
	30/3		Harassing fire demonstration at the front short 300 country cover an working party for signals 5th Inf Bde relieves 99th Inf Bde 2 Bdes as Reserve Brigade	Hulluch appdx 1/12 RA E.m.g. gro 2 3" gro HS
	31/3		No change	HS

Army Form C. 2118.

WAR DIARY
or
INTELLIGENCE SUMMARY.

(Erase heading not required.)

At 9 23GW

Vol 72

War Diary
A & Q Branch
23rd Division
1st April
to
30 April

Wiltshire Regt
MX 0 M 9
23 Div

Army Form C. 2118.

WAR DIARY
or
INTELLIGENCE SUMMARY.
(Erase heading not required.)

Instructions regarding War Diaries and Intelligence Summaries are contained in F. S. Regs., Part II and the Staff Manual respectively. Title pages will be prepared in manuscript.

Place	Date	Hour	Summary of Events and Information	Remarks and references to Appendices
SAINS en GOHELLE	1st April		No change	
	2 Ap		30 men fur tor extension of the Tourcoing (?) (176 (?) for mg camp	App 1
			6" Inf. B de 2" Div relieve 5" Doy B de 2" Div in the trench/reserve	App 2
			2 /t and 68 " Imp B Hv. every one reinforced village	App 2
	3 Ap		GOC 19 Army presented mitrailleuse pieces to Sthresse men 2.5 frs	App 2
	4 Ap		No change	App 2
	5 Ap		48 men per batt. are attached to the 176 Tournoing (?) for work.	App 2
	6 Ap		Internal reliefs sec 2 /t and 68 " Inf. B de	App 3
	7 Ap		No change	App 3
	8 Ap		"	App 3
	9 Ap		"	App 3
			Drafts received during week 14 L O R Standards for covering entrance to dug outs sent to be sent as a reminder to 1 at exchanging on cavalry or attacks	
			Internal reliefs in 68 and 69 B Ve	App 4

2353 Wt. W23141/1454 700,000 5/15 D. D. & L. A.D.S.S./Forms/C. 2118

WAR DIARY
or
INTELLIGENCE SUMMARY.
(Erase heading not required.)

Army Form C. 2118.

Instructions regarding War Diaries and Intelligence Summaries are contained in F. S. Regs., Part II. and the Staff Manual respectively. Title pages will be prepared in manuscript.

Place	Date	Hour	Summary of Events and Information	Remarks and references to Appendices
SAINS en GOHELLE	11/4/15		Orders received for relief of 1st 23rd Bde by 2nd Bde & for detachment of one 13th escort & section R.E. to PERNES ahead of move of main division. A.D.M.S. 1st Division inspected the 2nd Bn 4th 1st & 7th Royal 7/15th Manchesters	
	12/4		Nothing. Series of divisions inspected by G.O.C 1st Army. Notice received that we now i/c 1st Inf Div Staff appear Inf. Bde	
	13/4		6th Inf Bde & 2nd Bde relieved by 5th & 9th Inf Bde 250 men from division sent to 176th Tunnelling Coy Northumb and 181st 182nd R.E. to Division relieved by 13th W.R. 2nd Division	
	14/4		No Bands to PERNES – Reinforcements received during week. Officers 6 & OR	
	15/4		Relief of 23rd Bde by 2nd Strath Entrenchment – 69th Bde to HERSIN our billets	
	16/4		1st 2nd 5th Inf 13th Bde 69th 13th Bde move to DIVISION – 24th 13th move to HERSIN on relief by 99th 24th 13th	
	17/4		24 13th move to BRUAY. 63rd 13th move to HERSIN on relief of 6th Inf 13th	
	18/4		Scheme for move of Division on receiving orders for ready to goods and trains	

Army Form C. 2118.

WAR DIARY
or
INTELLIGENCE SUMMARY.
(Erase heading not required.)

Instructions regarding War Diaries and Intelligence Summaries are contained in F. S. Regs., Part II. and the Staff Manual respectively. Title pages will be prepared in manuscript.

Place	Date	Hour	Summary of Events and Information	Remarks and references to Appendices
	18"		Orders received - Division proceeds to C.I.A. & trazer under Lietels	
			2 nothing of special service note and movement	
			Positions of 23" Div. Transmitting (?) so that establishment is	No
			17.6" Tun. Con and Engineers ready to commence	
BRUAY	19"		Received A.D.M.S. order to BRUAY	
			R.A. of 23rd Div. less one bde R and one others relieved by A.A.R. ats.	
				(2135)
			1M.T proceed as for in 1 Cav. Div at SAMER for training	
			6.9" - 13" move to LAIRES area for training	
			Comp. working parties again Wire Division	No
	20."		No change - Baths recreation rooms and theatres started at	
			the new area	
			Rejoining of BRUAY from Front and certain pure during Training are LAIRES from Guns	No
	21st		No change NHD	
			No change NS	

2353 Wt. W2544/1454 700,000 5/15 D. D. & L. A.D.S.S./Forms/C. 2118

Army Form C. 2118.

WAR DIARY
or
INTELLIGENCE SUMMARY.

(Erase heading not required.)

Place	Date	Hour	Summary of Events and Information	Remarks and references to Appendices
BRUAY	23/6		No change.	
	24		Gas demonstration witnessed. Every man being sent through a room heavily charged with poisonous gas.	
			No change. Status quo on 13,23, 171 enemy men reported standby etc.	
	25		disinfected - trenches intact front.	
			No change	
	26		69th Bde over to HERSIN med. C. 68 Amb Division med. — 24 B'ed Trench	
			area	
	27		No change	
	28		No change	
	29		No change	
	30		No change	

Heathcoat, Col.
A.D.M.S.
23rd Division

1/5/16

WAR DIARY
or
INTELLIGENCE SUMMARY.

(Erase heading not required.)

Army Form C. 2118.

Four Field
A.S.C. Personnel
3rd Division

1st May 1916
to
31st May 1916

Villers IX

Army Form C. 2118.

WAR DIARY
or
INTELLIGENCE SUMMARY.
(Erase heading not required.)

Instructions regarding War Diaries and Intelligence Summaries are contained in F. S. Regs., Part II. and the Staff Manual respectively. Title pages will be prepared in manuscript.

Place	Date	Hour	Summary of Events and Information	Remarks and references to Appendices
BRUAY	May 1st		101° 7°C.Y. move from RUITZ to BULLY	
		102° " " " FOSSE 10 to RUITZ	
			New site selected for F.d Ambulance at BRUAY	
			25 Officers and 24 O.R. arrived. Little work or improvements	
	2 May		No change	
	3 May		No change	
			Army Commander presented 3 D.C.M. 3 M.M. to M.S.O. and men of the Division	
	4 May		9th Siege Coy.pers. (aus 1 C.M.) annexaft A front line in a working party 3 D.C.M. 3 M.M. to HERSIN area = 58°18 to Barring area by 1st	
	5 May		Montchougan 24.5th moves to DIVISION area	
			No change	
	6 May		Drafts received 3 officers and 8 O.R.	
	7 May		No change	
			Divisional staff with various Cos for demonstration	
	8 May		No change	
			Conference reference relief of 2nd Div. now held to be	

Army Form C. 2118.

WAR DIARY
or
INTELLIGENCE SUMMARY.
(Erase heading not required.)

Instructions regarding War Diaries and Intelligence Summaries are contained in F. S. Regs., Part II. and the Staff Manual respectively. Title pages will be prepared in manuscript.

Place	Date	Hour	Summary of Events and Information	Remarks and references to Appendices
BRUAY	9 May		102nd Fd Co. RE moved from RUITZ to FOSSE 10	App
"	10 May		128th " " " " RUITZ to FOSSE 10 & RUITZ	
"	"		24th Infy Bde moved from HERSIN area to SOUCHEZ section of line	App
"	11th May		69th " " " " and PERNES (town) to HERSIN area	App
"	12 "		69th " " " " HERSIN Area to ANGRES section	App
SAINS-EN- GOHELLE	13 "		Div Headquarters moved from BRUAY to SAINS-en-GOHELLE. Reinforcements received during week 50 Off; 1510 O.R. Scheme for Reorganization R.A. received. New site for treatment of baths in BOUVIGNY inspected w/3 BOUVIGNY wood	App
"	14 "		68th Mach Gun Co. moved from VINCLY to BARLIN	App
"	15 "		" " " " " BARLIN to SOUCHEZ section	App
"	16 "		" " " " " SOUCHEZ Sector & LORETTE Ridge.	App
"	"		2/4 " " bytrain from PERNES & BARLIN. 20 Off 1510 OR from DACH	
"	17 "		12th Durham L.I. bytrain from PERNES & BARLIN. 20 Off 1510 OR from DACH	
"	18 "		Started by road for CALAIS	
"	"		12th Durham L.I. from BARLIN to NOTRE DAME DE LORETTE.	
"	"		2 Off 12 40 OR DAC left by train for CALAIS. Weekly conference held at 5 pm.	App
"	19 "		H.Q. and 3 batts 68th J. Bde moved by rail from PERNES to HERSIN. Supplies wagons + Harness from R.A. on reorganization despatched by rail from BARLIN to CALAIS	App

2353 Wt. W2544/1454 700,000 5/15 D.D.&L. A.D.S.S./Forms/C. 2118.

Army Form C. 2118.

WAR DIARY
or
INTELLIGENCE SUMMARY.
(Erase heading not required.)

Instructions regarding War Diaries and Intelligence Summaries are contained in F.S. Regs., Part II. and the Staff Manual respectively. Title pages will be prepared in manuscript.

Place	Date	Hour	Summary of Events and Information	Remarks and references to Appendices
GOHELLE	20th		No change except that 68/3 in reserve, 24 July 10½	M2
	21st		HQ 2 Bde now at FRESNICOURT and HQ 2 in 13/4 to HERSIN moving to 44.7 - 220.2	
			Army recognised 1/4 3 rd Bde 2 - 0th	
			Our guns L102 RFA destroyed by shell fire	
			Reinforcement received during preceding month 21 officers 322 men	
			B103 - B108 - D104 B⁴ RFA raised up into the line from training at THIEULOYE	M2
	22nd		137th 2w 15th moved up from VERDREL to FOSSE II	M2
			2 Coy 1st Staffords back to 44.7 - Bde 2	M2
	23rd		One gun A103 FRA damaged	M2
	24th		D104 one 4.5 How fell not Baden by premature	M2
	25th		2 Lt. 1st Staffords back to 47-Sw. 1 return	M2
			1 gun A104 B⁴ RFA pd out to Bartoca	M2
	26th		No change	M2
	28th		No 11 Labour Bn Line 3 Coy gone division for work class 1 (b) wound assessed Home 69°-7A, rear bank, No Engrs to be loan for support at YPRES	M2
			70-7A " " - Lieut J BARRIN	
			71-7A " " - Maison RUITZ	

2353 Wt. W2544/1454 700,000 5/15 D.D.&L. A.D.S.S./Forms/C.2118.

Army Form C. 2118.

WAR DIARY
or
INTELLIGENCE SUMMARY.
(Erase heading not required.)

Instructions regarding War Diaries and Intelligence Summaries are contained in F. S. Regs., Part II. and the Staff Manual respectively. Title pages will be prepared in manuscript.

Place	Date	Hour	Summary of Events and Information	Remarks and references to Appendices
SAINSar GOHELLE	28"		Transport animals moved out BEUVRY LA and Sous LE FROISSART	
	29"		First "D" Branch moved to BARLIN - then the remains at GOHELLE per vehicles moved out of POSN 10 & brick of billeting area 3 of company	
RUITZ	30"		2 Coys & M.G.s moved up to GOHELLE	
		6.a. 13 a	arrived by 2.4 . 13 a	#2
			New Transport arrived & received fresh horses and 10 officers 211 men	
	31"		Information to hand that transport are only able to work against soft ground. Conference at Advanced H.Q. at 6.P.M. an we not provided with horses. I suppose but that south arching we are and this confusion may arise no orders again & extra tents and this confusion may arise	#2

Hutchinson Lt Col
Asst P. O. B.
23 Division

2353 Wt. W2544/1454 700,000 5/15 D. D. & L. A.D.S.S./Forms/C. 2118.

Army Form C. 2118.

WAR DIARY
INTELLIGENCE SUMMARY.
(Erase heading not required.)

War Diary
"A" & "Q" Branch
23rd Division
1st June 1916
to
30th June 1916

Army Form C. 2118.

WAR DIARY
or
INTELLIGENCE SUMMARY.
(Erase heading not required.)

Instructions regarding War Diaries and Intelligence Summaries are contained in F. S. Regs., Part II. and the Staff Manual respectively. Title pages will be prepared in manuscript.

Place	Date	Hour	Summary of Events and Information	Remarks and references to Appendices
BARLIN	1/8/16		Hostile actions for preceding month 11 missing 4 S killed 23 wounded (3 Officers Killed (4) Officers wounded)	
			Self-inflicted wounds for " " 3 Officers 18 OR	
			Reinforcements received for " " 63 " 10+3 OR	
			10 1/2 Divisions sighted. Hostile artillery active in area	
			Enemy artillery has ranged on our camp last 3 nights	
			Sunday evening (enemy) heavy gunner shell 1 90 c.m 5" military motor	
			Head Quarter 24 Inf Bde destroyed 10 shell fire - aircraft detected no Bully Grenay	
	2/8/16		at R 11 + B 4	
	3/8/16		No change	
	4/8/16		10.30 A.M. R.M. Bni arrived in area related for arrangements and survey	
			10.45 - 12.0 ?	
			Brit. Inf. area for following persons assembled R 23 d.2.2	
			1 C.O.	
			1 CM.G.	
			2 H.O.	
			4 Military Pers	
			1 Medical	
			6 C.M	
			8 "	
			10 Infantry details	

Army Form C. 2118.

WAR DIARY
or
INTELLIGENCE SUMMARY.
(Erase heading not required.)

Instructions regarding War Diaries and Intelligence
Summaries are contained in F.S. Regs., Part II.
and the Staff Manual respectively. Title pages
will be prepared in manuscript.

Place	Date	Hour	Summary of Events and Information	Remarks and references to Appendices
BARLIN	4/6/16		Reinforcements received for force consisting of 2 S/Officers & 114 N/rs & ranks.	
	5/6/16		No change.	
	6/6/16		No change except the D. Squadron returned to HQ.	
GOHELLE	7/6/15		No change.	
	8/6/16		Reliefs of 68", 3rd 0/a by 69", 13" on night of 8th before. 1/4 Hus 13" R.W Division joins us for training. Orders for move by 2,3" June to HQ received on relief by 47" & R.N Divs are at.	
	9/6/15		Relief by 69" & 68" Bn completed. Capt R.B.G.LAWRENCE I/W/N R. attached to 2/3 N/Y Staffs Regt. Reinforcements received by various locations to facilitate march 1 S/Officers 37 O.R. Res 1/5 " 2/8 " 1/5 " 1/5 " 6/7 "N.Staffords attached to 2/3rd W. Staffords on the strength to. 4E CM retaining commenced. relieve of RE 47" Division in the Franspran	
	11/6/16		62" Bn/1/4 released by 141 & 9" Bn RFA & 7" Division 9" Bn Staffords moved back to CAMBLAIN	

2353 Wt W25411/1454 700,000 5/15 D. D. & L. A.D.S.S./Forms/C. 2118.

WAR DIARY
or
INTELLIGENCE SUMMARY.
(Erase heading not required.)

Army Form C. 2118.

Place	Date	Hour	Summary of Events and Information	Remarks and references to Appendices
GOHELLE	12/6/16		68" Inf Bde move to LISBOURG area	
			2/4" - relived by 140" Bde 47 Div and move to HERSIN area	
			RE relief completed and move to LA THIEULOYE	
			Relief B Field Ambulances commence	
			Police posts relieved	
			PERNES	
	13/6		2/4" Bde move to THIEPVAL area	
			69" Bde relieved by 47" Div move to HERSIN area	
			191 names submitted for military medal	
BRUAY	14/6		69" Bde to DIVISION area	
			Div HQ to BRUAY	
			Capt C J WALLACE appointed B'de Major 68" Bde 13" Div vice Lord Dudley Gordon	
			A/Lieut Colonel 10" N.F.	
			Major MOORE 6802 knocked down & ridden by G.O.C. Recon Army as per	
			move down	
			Battle casualties during front's Mars killed 7 wounded - OR 11 missing 85 killed	
			4 2 C recommended	

Army Form C. 2118.

WAR DIARY
or
INTELLIGENCE SUMMARY.
(Erase heading not required.)

Instructions regarding War Diaries and Intelligence Summaries are contained in F. S. Regs., Part II. and the Staff Manual respectively. Title pages will be prepared in manuscript.

Place	Date	Hour	Summary of Events and Information	Remarks and references to Appendices
BRUAY	15/3/16		58th Divn. moved into DELETTE area. Artillery relieved by 47th Art and moved to MIELLE and CLARQUES area. T.M. Batteries (motored) sent off to ST POL	
BOMY	16/3		Divl. HQ & 1st mop. to BOMY	
			2 & 13 th " to FLECHIN area	
			69th B de " " ESTRE-BLANCHE area	
			R.A. " " CLARQUES area	
			Pioneers " " BEAUMETZ IN AIRES	
			R.E " " MATRINGHEM	
			73 Amb " " B/refett areas	
	17/6		Orders received for division to form reserve army formation, the man Gemmatis Corps	
	18/6		2nd C.Q. HAN DCCK, 1 & 2 LS attached to Divl HQ vice Capt LAWRENCE attached to Bdy HQ on the Staff of Brigadier Commander changed	
	19/5		Division to form part of 3 2nd Corps. Int of A. Stedman changed.	

Army Form C. 2118.

WAR DIARY
or
INTELLIGENCE SUMMARY.
(Erase heading not required.)

Instructions regarding War Diaries and Intelligence Summaries are contained in F.S. Regs., Part II. and the Staff Manual respectively. Title pages will be prepared in manuscript.

Place	Date	Hour	Summary of Events and Information	Remarks and references to Appendices
BONNY	20/6/16		Orders received for advanced parties to go to AILLY sur SOMME S.A.A. for twenty guns for which transport not to proceed to be returned to Railhead r/y 44 train for on.	
	21/6		Advanced parties under Major O.M.G. proceed to AILLY	
	22/6		Training time table received	
	23/6		No change	
VAUX en AMIENOIS	24/6		Bie. H.Q. arrived by car. Troops commence entraining. Infantry first then R.E. & Ambulances No three R.A. Two Officers left behind (2ⁿᵈ in C and others) at entraining area at detraining station (650's and Dathech) stations. Generally supervising. Troops continue to arrive.	
	25/6			

2353 Wt W2344/1454 700,000 5/15 D.D.&L. A.D.S.S./Forms/C. 2118.

Army Form C. 2118.

WAR DIARY
or
INTELLIGENCE SUMMARY.
(Erase heading not required.)

Place	Date	Hour	Summary of Events and Information	Remarks and references to Appendices
	26/6		Last troops arrive	MS
	27/6		Orders received for move into RAINEVILLE area	MS
			- movement in strip known	
	28/6		Orders for move cancelled	MS
	29/6		Orders to be prepared to move to RAINEVILLE area received.	MS
	30/6		Move of division except this H.Q. commence at 3.30 pm.	MS

Heilly recovery 1877
A.A.Q.M.G.
2 3rd Division

A + Q

23rd /Div n

July 1916

23 July

A&Q 23 D 3

Vol. 10

War Diary
A & Q Branches
2nd Division
1st July 1916
to
31st July 1916

Army Form C. 2118.

349

WAR

INTELLIGEN[CE]
(Erase head)

Instructions regarding War Diaries and Intelligence Summaries are contained in F. S. Regs., Part II. and the Staff Manual respectively. Title pages will be prepared in manuscript.

Place	Date	Hour	Summary of Events and Information	Remarks and references to Appendices
VAUX en AMIENOIS	1/7/16		Bn. [Rein?]forcement received storing/Browns month Officers – 82 & 1 W	the rank & file 1717 W
			Total balloted: also	1103
			That[?] rec'd admissions	
			Immediate rewards granted:	" 31 — 941
				M. C. 4 A.C.M 3 M.M 23
				C.B.1 — C.M.G.1 — D.S.O 2 — M.C 4 — M1
				D.C.M 2 — M.M 11
			Honours and awards to	
			Service system employed – the avenue and [?] field at the
			same time 28/29 troops lift at M.M 28/29 m 27 Infantry
			Same time og. lorries lift at M.M m 30 x 81. m
			trains lift M.M at 5.0 p.m 29 where troops were entrained & conveyed
			as by trains themof. lorries reached rendez vous point
			4.30 hours from Methel in 7.30/8.30 troops to units by march route
			4.30 [?] from Methel on night 7/8 M.M troops to units by march route
			to stations m 31 commencing 3/7
			For attack on [second?] line forced at M.M 17/23
			via G.H.Q. reserve ready to move at 1 hour notice.
			Order received at 5.30 p.m to move to area South East of SIGNAT EN
			Inf to BAIZIEUX Area – Troops commenced moving at 8.0 pm

WAR DIARY or INTELLIGENCE SUMMARY

Army Form C. 2118.

Place	Date	Hour	Summary of Events and Information	Remarks and references to Appendices
BAIZIEUX	2 July		The attack so far not very successful.	
			Ammn rentrial at CONTÉ	
			Supply " . VIGNACOURT	
			Refilling on BAIZIEUX - FRANCVILLERS road.	
			100 hand carts arrive for decoro from detachments	
			4 p.m. Ordered to be prepared to move eastwards	
			5.45 p.m. Detailed orders received	
			6.45 p.m. Other orders cancelling 5.45 p.m. orders rec'd - Placed under III Corps.	
			Div H.Q. formerie 24th Bde & R.A. to remain - 68th Bde to MILLENCOURT - 69 to underlying pos	
			Divn - Pioneers road & Coy R.E. to BELLEVUE FARM	350
	3 July		No change	
VIVIER MILL	4 July		H.Q. 187 R.E. 24th B.G. move to DERNANCOURT area	
			68th Bde to BECOURT wood - 2 & 3rd line back to E.9.A	
			69th Bde engaged in small operations	
			24th Bde placed at disposal of 19th Divn	
			Gen Artillery relief of 34th Div ordered	
			" " " cancelled	

Army Form C. 2118.

WAR DIARY
or
INTELLIGENCE SUMMARY.
(Erase heading not required.)

Place	Date	Hour	Summary of Events and Information	Remarks and references to Appendices
VIVIER MILL	5/7		2 Trench Mortar Batteries from B.N. Division to join division temporarily (225 & m.l.)	
		3	" " " from 38" Div " " "	
			Inniskilling and Yeomanry withdrawn from front line and ordered to clear up grounds and yeomanry withdrawn from front line and ordered to clear up	
			2 Officers 50 men 8th Staffords to work tram line	
			1 Officer 60 " - for salvage	
			2 Coys - for carrying grenades	
			Showered forward upon up to 19th Div front in early morning	
			68th B[de] told to send 115 2/7th BECOURT wood as it was ground they	
			had withdrawn 3.10 relieved by 2	
			2 Coy R.E.(Div) attached to Division	
			1 sec 86 R.A. " " " mens up	
			" " AA 35 "	
			69" and 24" heavily engaged. Up to date 190 German prisoners	
			taken.	
			Casualties 3 officers killed 2 wounded O.R. 4 killed 15 wounded	
			69" B[de] relieved by 68" Inf B[de]	
6/7			Orders received for attack operations on morning 7th	
			Casualties for 6th Officers killed 7 wounded 27 Infantry 1	
			O.R. — 19 " — 197	

Army Form C. 2118.

WAR DIARY
or
INTELLIGENCE SUMMARY.
(Erase heading not required.)

Place	Date	Hour	Summary of Events and Information	Remarks and references to Appendices
VIVIER MILL	7/6		6.8° B⁺ C⁺ on left of line hand over part of their line to 50ᵗʰ Inf Bde 19ᵗʰ Div. 2.4ᵗʰ B⁺ take over movement to right from 52ⁿᵈ B⁺ᵈᵉ 17ᵗʰ Bris. 6.9 B⁺ᵈᵉ in reserve near VIVIER MILL. Engineer stores and bomb dumps and ammunition dumps organized to feed three Brigades - water - ration - grenade - R.E. store carrying parties organized. Trans train and organized. Attack delivered by 68' × 24' guns together but at 8.06 pr 24". Attack delivered by 68' × 24' guns together but at 8.06 pr 24"— direction out of CONTALMAISON. Wet weather again made all emergency roads impracticable even for empty vehicles. One metalled road traffic out of repair is only one workable — 6.9° B⁺ᵈᵉ complimented on behaviour by Corps Commander for fighting on 6ᵗʰ. 2.4ᵗʰ B⁺ᵈᵉ complimented by Army Commander on taking CONTALMAISON. Four 4" stokes mortars B.M. Sec M.C⁷ attached to Bris. Stokes carrying party 0/9 from 34ᵗʰ Bris arrived 11.0 a.m; Tmy	75/2

WAR DIARY or INTELLIGENCE SUMMARY

Army Form C. 2118.

Place	Date	Hour	Summary of Events and Information	Remarks and references to Appendices
	8/7		were withdrawn again at 5.30 pm and men C 79's were handed and left out onward. System of supply of grenades altered to be reorganised.	
			Casualties on 7th Officers killed 6 wounded 21 missing 1	
			O.R. " 26 " 434 " 53	
			Heavy rain all day	
			Very heavy rain makes all sick tracks impassable	
			Casualties on 8th Officers killed 10 wounded 21 missing 4	
			O.R. " 111 " 372 " 169	
	9/7		Bright	
			2nd Lt EDEN DSO & Brooks arrived to assume command of 2nd Bn 15th	
			Orders received that 1st Div return as on night of 9/10th.	
			Prisoners confirmed dispersion up to date 217	

Place	Date	Hour	Summary of Events and Information	Remarks and references to Appendices
VIVIER MILL	10/6		Casualties - Officers - Killed 3 wounded 19 missing 1	
			O.R. " 24 " 452 " 87 Msg	
			Relief of 23rd Division by 1st Division commences	
			68 Bde to ALBERT	
			24" " to BRESLE	
			69" " to attack CONTALMAISON	
			R.A. remain	
			R.E. & R.A.M.C. exchange billets	
			68" Bde engaged	
			69" Bde captured CONTALMAISON about 6.0 p.m. heavy counter-	
			attacked about 10-0 p.m.	
			Casualties - Officers 5 wounded	
			O.R. Killed 13 wounded 112 missing 15	
			Carrying parties had great difficulty in getting stores up owing	
			to gas shells and barrage.	

Army Form C. 2118.

WAR DIARY
or
INTELLIGENCE SUMMARY.
(Erase heading not required.)

Instructions regarding War Diaries and Intelligence Summaries are contained in F. S. Regs., Part II. and the Staff Manual respectively. Title pages will be prepared in manuscript.

Place	Date	Hour	Summary of Events and Information	Remarks and references to Appendices
ST GRATIEN	11/7		Div: H.Q.'s now heads to ST GRATIEN. 9th Staffords and Dublops Company up as to last stated 9th Staffords have received up to last stated 33 prisoners and Lewis Gun – 310 bodies buried including 33 prisoners. General OXLEY came to 2nd Inf Bde Head qt 1 for Col EDEN. Total captures by 69th Inf & 13th = 9 machine guns 5 T.M. and 21 men. 69th Bde relieved by 13th of 1st Division. Casualties officers – killed 1 wounded 4 missing 2 OR " 16 " 141 "	
	12/7		Army Commander sends congratulatory wire on capture amounts of CONTAL MAISON and behaviour of troops 33rd bodies (Doches) 1 & 2 bodies German buried 2nd Inf Bde move to PIERREGOT – MIRVAUX Was 193(M) M.P.(M) and 198(M) move to BAFILE Wood Casualties Officers 13 Killed 28 wounded 1 missing OR 33 " 600 " 159 "	

WAR DIARY
or
INTELLIGENCE SUMMARY.
(Erase heading not required.)

Army Form C. 2118.

Place	Date	Hour	Summary of Events and Information	Remarks and references to Appendices
			Bodies buried British 126. Germans 64	25.6
			Total casualties during fighting	
			Officers killed 167	
			O.R. " missing 3481	
			24" Bde 48 Officers 1135 O.R.	
			68" " 26 " 773 "	
			69" " 73 " 1358 "	
			Showery	
			910	
	13/7		69" Bde and 101 Coy R.E. moved back to MOLLIENS aux SOIS	
			24" " 12" " proceed to & prepared to entrain and be disbanded	
			68" 70" " Inf Bde "	
			Bodies buried British 200 German 88	
			Showery	

Army Form C. 2118.

WAR DIARY
or
INTELLIGENCE SUMMARY.
(Erase heading not required.)

Place	Date	Hour	Summary of Events and Information	Remarks and references to Appendices
	14/7		2/4" Bde move to POULAINVILLE - Signal Section and Hdqrs company are out to go with Brigade - Bde transferred to 8th Division 68th Inf Bde ordered to cooperate with 34th Bde? Bodies buried 19 British 4 Germans. Casualties 1 OR wounded 11 OR wounded. Showery	
	15/7		2/4 Inf Bde commence to entrain at 11.0 a.m. and join 8 Division 70 Inf Bde from 8" Div to join 23 Div? Bodies buried British 165 Germans 98 Casualties 1 wounded Heavy rain	
	16/7		70 Bde commence entraining at 9.0 a.m. and billet at POULAINVILLE 9 N.S. Staffords return to ST GRETIEN Salvage to ALBERT Bearer sub. division 71st ? Amb attached to 103 F.A. at ALBERT More rain. Bodies buried - British 197 German 91	
	17/7		70" Bde move to PIERREGOT and MIRVAUX 68" Inf Bde heavily employed	

Army Form C. 2118.

WAR DIARY
or
INTELLIGENCE SUMMARY.
(Erase heading not required.)

Instructions regarding War Diaries and Intelligence Summaries are contained in F. S. Regs. Part II. and the Staff Manual respectively. Title pages will be prepared in manuscript.

Place	Date	Hour	Summary of Events and Information	Remarks and references to Appendices
	17/7		Total bodies buried by 23 Bde. 1518 British 410 Germans Heavy rain most of the day. About 2,000 rifles, 3 M. guns, 3 Lewis 3 T. mortars and other articles as ammunition salved.	
	18/7		Train company and 1 Horse Transport 68" Inf Bde, Hq Trench M. and 2 be 3 be men ever 500 to get into new 3 Corps area. Staffs for Brigades very resourceful factory. Men of all sorts of units sent to B's - large number of Bantams sent 59 Yorks 55% of whom are to be returned to base as unsuitable type except for ever - Personnel of 23" Bde T.M. Bgr (Medium) return and stores of 38" Bde received Moves cancelled Due 16 pr. horses and guns Showing - 6 officers killed 5 wounded OR. killed at 14/7, wounded 666 ½, Dec ½ Connecticut 3rd Yorkshire missing. 68" 3rd 13" received during night and go to ALBERT Casualties 1 R. Fus. 13 Division list R.M.	#22 #23
	19/7			

Army Form C. 2118.

WAR DIARY
or
INTELLIGENCE SUMMARY.
(Erase heading not required.)

Instructions regarding War Diaries and Intelligence Summaries are contained in F. S. Regs., Part II. and the Staff Manual respectively. Title pages will be prepared in manuscript.

359

Place	Date	Hour	Summary of Events and Information	Remarks and references to Appendices
	20/7		9. O.C. presented ribbons to 69th and 13th wounded recruits for July 3rd 1918.	
			22 more military medals awarded	
			Casualties R.A. 5 wounded	
			Bright warm day	
			68th Inf. B de. move to FRANVILLERS	No
HÉNENCOURT	21/7		New H.Q. move to Chateau HÉNENCOURT — R.A. remain vie Bois Laviée - 68° D who not move	
			69th "B" de. move to MILLENCOURT — 70th 13th to BAIZIEUX wood - Train & BRIGADE	
			R.E. 2 Coy MILLENCOURT 1 Coy BAIZIEUX - 7 Amb. BAIZIEUX - BÉVINCOURT - MILLENCOURT	
			Use. Salvage Coy and Supply Column & M.G.C. de. do not move.	
			G.O.C. presented 44 Military medals to 68° & 69° Bdes wounded recruits	
			for July 5" to 12th	
			Hot day	
			Casualties O.R. 4 killed 27 wounded all artillery	No
	22/7		71° & 4° Amt. move to BELCOURT CHATEAU	
			division ordered to be ready to move at 1 hour notice	
			23 Military Medals awarded to recruits to 24" to 13th for & to 11 July	

Date	Hour	Summary of Events and Information	Remarks and references to Appendices
22nd / 1m+		Dull cold day. Casualties R.A. 4 killed 11 wounded	
23/7		23rd S.H.E. and wagon lines moved to E3c and E2d S1W of ALBERT. Ammunition replenishment E3D BELLEVUE F^m E3C. Casualties 1 Officer wounded 14 OR wounded R.A	M.O.
24/7		Dull day. Orders received for 23rd Div. to relieve 1st Div. Transfer of drafts to their proper units within the division took place. Batteries not required to be sent away. Still not fine. Casualties 6 killed 13 wounded R.A	M.O.
25/7		70th + 13th move up next June via relief B 1" B 2". Dull day. Cloudy/fine	7:20

WAR DIARY or INTELLIGENCE SUMMARY

Army Form C. 2118.

Place	Date	Hour	Summary of Events and Information	Remarks and references to Appendices
ALBERT	26/7		3rd HQ move to ALBERT	
			68 - 13th take over from from 3rd Bde	
			69 - 13 - to Albert	
			R.E. & A.S. moved relieve each other in 23rd & 1st Bdes	
			R.A. remain in line	
			2 Military medals awarded 69th YA & 101st 7th M	148
			Casualties 6 killed 39 wounded	
			Still very annoying	
	27/7		3 Military medals awarded to RA	
			101 Co RE ALBERT 102 BECOURT wood 128 BECOURT wood	
			7A 69 FRICOURT 70 BAIZIEUX 71 BECOURT CHATEAU	
			9 - 5 Staj BECOURT wood	
			Reliefs continue 68 & 70 B.Rs	
			Hot day	1700
			Casualties Officers killed 1 wounded 4 missing 1	
			OR " 6 " 62 " 6	
	28/7		69 - 13th relieve 68 - 2nd 13th in the line	
			11 military medals awarded	

361

Army Form C. 2118.

WAR DIARY
or
INTELLIGENCE SUMMARY.
(Erase heading not required.)

Place	Date	Hour	Summary of Events and Information	Remarks and references to Appendices
J 27 c 55 Shirt S7D	29/7		Shelled out of camp which was heavily bombarded 8" 9.2" 12" Casualties Officers 1 wounded OR 15 killed 88 wounded 10 missing	262
			Hot day	H22
			5.30 - HQ shelled - move to a camp 1/4 mile west of ALBERT. Casualties Officers wounded 11 missing 2 OR Killed 18 Wounded 142 missing 16	
			Hot day Establish a large water dump near Central Renson villa	H22
	30/7		No change Hot day Casualties Officers 3 killed 13 wounded 1 missing OR 9 " 107 " 2 "	
			Hot day	

Army Form C. 2118.

WAR DIARY
or
INTELLIGENCE SUMMARY.
(Erase heading not required.)

Place	Date	Hour	Summary of Events and Information	Remarks and references to Appendices
	31/7		No change. Water supply damaged, practically none available at BECURT. Arranged a new scheme north and of 9 water wagons. Casualties Hot day. Warned we move 50 into reserve the 6" and go north on 8" Officers Killed 1 Wounded 12 OR " 34 " 208 Missing 51 Headcount TL Officers 5 OR 203	

23rd Division

A & Q.

23rd DIVISION.

AUGUST 1916

Army Form C. 2118.

WAR DIARY
INTELLIGENCE SUMMARY.
(Erase heading not required.)

A & Q

Vol 11

War Diary
A & Q Branches
23rd Division
1 August 1916
to
31 August 1916

Volume XII

Hurtbecourg Tor
N+ P.m.g
23-31

WAR DIARY or INTELLIGENCE SUMMARY

Army Form C. 2118.

Place	Date	Hour	Summary of Events and Information	Remarks and references to Appendices
Camp W27 C66 Sh51 57D	1st Aug 16		**Battle** Casualties during month Officers 212 OR 4461	
			Reinforcements " " 138 Officers 2862 OR	
			Sick " " 28 Officers 709 OR	
			Convalescents returned " M & 3 MM 71	
			10" N.F. relieve 11 W.Y.	
			13" D.L.I. " 8 Yorks	
			68" S.M. D.M. TM Bty relieve those of 69" Inf Bde	
			11" N.F. relieve 8" K.O.Y.L.I.	
			12 " D.L.I " 8 Y & L	
			Casualties Officers 2 wounded at duty	
			O.R 4 killed 67 wounded	Apx
			Hot day	
	2nd Aug		No change - 2 Winter Stories sent to Divn	
			Casualties - Officers 4 wounded	
			O.R 12 killed 57 wounded	Apx

WAR DIARY
or
INTELLIGENCE SUMMARY.
(Erase heading not required.)

Place	Date	Hour	Summary of Events and Information	Remarks and references to Appendices
	3/8/16		ALBERT heavily shelled. Staff Captain HURD-WOOD killed - Capt A E E LOWRY 2 wounded appointed Staff Capt. Casualties Officers 4 wounded O.R 7 killed 50 wounded 4 missing	
	4/9		Hot day. G.P Staff A/Cpl captured a machine gun. 2.3 M.M commenced a successful attack on German trenches but were driven out by M.G. un Fire 68 Inf Bde delivered a successful attack on German trenches but were driven out by M.G. un Fire Casualties 5 killed 4 wounded (Officers) " 11 " 58 " 3 missing (O.R) Cold dull day. Orders received to be prepared to move to BRESLE - FRANVILLERS - LA HOUSSOYE - BEHENCOURT area on 7th and entrain on 11th	

WAR DIARY
INTELLIGENCE SUMMARY
(Erase heading not required.)

Army Form C. 2118.

Instructions regarding War Diaries and Intelligence Summaries are contained in F.S. Regs., Part II. and the Staff Manual respectively. Title pages will be prepared in manuscript.

367

Place	Date	Hour	Summary of Events and Information	Remarks and references to Appendices
	5/8/16		89th Bde to relieve 68th 13th Bde in the lines. Immediate rewards received 870 L, MC 9, DCM 11, MM 3. Cool bright day. Casualties Officers killed 3, wounded 2, missing 1 O.R. " 28 " 199 " 5	H/3
	6/8/16		Relief by 15th Division commenced on 7th. Immediate rewards received MC 5, DCM 1. Casualties Officers killed –, wounded 1, missing 6 O.R. " 30 " " " 24 Hot day	H/4
	7/8/16		46th Bnf. to relieve 70th 13 Bde to FRANVILLERS. 73rd–74th relieving 161st to FRANVILLERS. Casualties Officers killed 1, wounded 10, missing – O.R. " 22 " 95 " missing 6 Hot day	H/7

Place	Date	Hour	Summary of Events and Information	Remarks and references to Appendices
BAIZIEUX	8 Aug		Div Hd qrs moved to BAIZIEUX at 6.0 p.m after handing over to 15" Div	
			69" Inf 13th relieved by 45" 12th to BRESLE	
			68 " - " - 44" B.G.M to BEHENCOURT & LA HUSSOYE also 9" Inf Bgd	
			102 7th 9 relieved by 91st to BEHENCOURT	
			128 " - " - 7th to BRESLE	
			69" 7A to LAVIEVILLE - 70" BAIZIEUX - 71st to BEHENCOURT	
			Casualties Officers wounded 1	
			OR Killed 5 wounded 21	
			Hot day	
			Immediate rewards granted 1 M.C. 1 D.C.M	M.22
	9 Aug		No change	
			2M & 9M.G. and tubing parties leave for BAIZIEUX	
			9 it Div" distributed medal ribbons to 68 Inf Bgde	
			Hot day	
	10 Aug		Transport proceeds by road to ALLONVILLE - CARDONETTE & POULAINVILLE	
			G.9 & Div" distributed medal ribbons to 69" Inf 13th	
			Immediate rewards awarded 8 D.S.O. for mayr Hrenne Gray	
			Advanced parties leave for x temp area about AILLY le HAUT CLOCHER tois morning	M.23

Army Form C. 2118.

WAR DIARY
or
INTELLIGENCE SUMMARY.
(Erase heading not required.)

Place	Date	Hour	Summary of Events and Information	Remarks and references to Appendices
AILLY LE HAUT CLOCHER	11 Aug		Div H.Q. move to AILLY and come under X'n Corps	
			68' Bde 102 F.A Coy 71' F.A to GORENFLOS and AILLY - GORENFLOS - ERGNIES - FAMECHIN	
			69" – 128 F° Coy 69' FA + VAUCHELLES – VAUCHELLES - VAUCOURT - BELLANCOURT - BUIGNY	
			70" – 101 F°Coy 70 FA – PONTREMY – PONTREMY - FRANCIERES - COCQUEREL	
			Train Companies moved with Div	
			Mob vessels R.A. remain on train	
			Divs Sigs and T.M. head cart detachments to	
			Troops supposed to start entraining at 0.55 am but trains 6½ hours late starting - 4 hours journey -	No 2
			Dull clear day.	
	12 Aug		Rest troops got into camps at 3.30 a.m.	
			Division commence entraining for BAILLEUL to join II Corps	
			68' and 70" Bdes commence entraining at 5.30 pm and 8.25 pm respectively.	
			Hot day	
			6 and infantry awarded.	

WAR DIARY or INTELLIGENCE SUMMARY

Army Form C. 2118.

Place	Date	Hour	Summary of Events and Information	Remarks and references to Appendices
FLETRE	13 Aug		Div. HQ to FLETRE arrived 9.0 p.m.	
			68th & 70th Bde. ordered to bivouac in area about CAESTRE and METEREN	
			Inspections	
			9th Corps rel passed & taking over from 5 Corps	
			Fine day	
	14 Aug		Retirement of Brit. two Art. completed by 1.0 p.m.	
			69 Inf Bde to area N of CAESTRE	
			70 Inf Bde moved up to STEENWERCK area also 7 Ambulance	
			H.M. The King met the Prince of WALES passed thro' area and stopped and CAESTRE	
			where met by GOC Div. met GOC 68th & 69th Inf Bde also BGRA + AA & QMG	
			Showery	
			Relief B 23rd Div 1st by 15th Bde Div Art commenced	Acw
	15 Aug		70 Bde relieved 122nd Brigade in bright sector area	
			68 Bde move to STEENWERCK area also 71st & 7 Amb	
			13 Fd Amb surrounded	

WAR DIARY
INTELLIGENCE SUMMARY

Army Form C. 2118.

Place	Date	Hour	Summary of Events and Information	Remarks and references to Appendices
			Arrangements made for taking over Trench stores, ammunition and general dumps - Traffic control posts - Water debris - Tramway lines - Tunnel wardens - Recreation rooms - Baths - Laundry - Drainage scheme.	
			A lot of work required in many of Cantonments - horse standings - shelters - drainage &c	
			Showery.	420
	16 Aug		M.G.C. Bde & T.M. Bty to Frelinghien	
			B.G. R.A. relieves 123rd Bde at LE BIZET & ARMENTIERS	
			9th Staffords relieves units to STEENWERCK area	
			101 R.F.A. LORIDAN 182 to DOUDOU 7m & 128 to PONT de NIEPPE taking over from 228, 237,233 (?)	
			71 & 79 take over from 139 FA at STEENWERCK	
			59 " " " 140 FA at PONT de NIEPPE	
			Light showers.	
			C.R.A. arrives from ALBERT	420
STEENWERCK	17 Aug		H.Q. HP move to STEENWERCK taking over area from 41st Division	
			R.A. arrive from ALBERT	

Army Form C. 2118.

WAR DIARY
or
INTELLIGENCE SUMMARY.
(Erase heading not required.)

Instructions regarding War Diaries and Intelligence Summaries are contained in F. S. Regs., Part II. and the Staff Manual respectively. Title pages will be prepared in manuscript.

372

Place	Date	Hour	Summary of Events and Information	Remarks and references to Appendices
	18/8		69* 18th moves up to STEENWERCK area	
			6.8* & 7.0* 18th to Armentières	
			9* 18th relieve 19* Middlesex	
			Showery	tw
			Schemes required for road repair, drainage, tramways, trenches, horse	
			standings, return dumps in trees, store & records etc to be rendered	
			in about 48 hour.	
			Heavy shower	
			Divi area changed	tw
	19/8		R.A. commence relief of R.A. 41st Div.?	
			Heavy shower	
			9 in I, and 9 SCMs awarded 70 Bde	tw
	20/8		R.A. relief continued	
			11 M.M.; awarded 6.8 - 13th	
			Heavy showers.	

Army Form C. 2118.

WAR DIARY
or
INTELLIGENCE SUMMARY.
(Erase heading not required.)

379

Place	Date	Hour	Summary of Events and Information	Remarks and references to Appendices
2.1 Fr	21/8		A A relief's changed unopposed. Conference - Method of wilding the line charged resulting in new billeting arrangements. Showery	
	22/8	17.00	G.O.C gave away medal ribbons to 63rd R^d	
			No change except establishment of a reinforcement camp. Area changed again S. Ancestry 8" Yorks and 10" Yorks relieve 10" N Riding and 11" West Yorks	M19
	23/8		Conference at Corps 2 billeting area. G.O.C Genl medal ribbons to R.A. & S. Staffords. Showery	M22
	24/8		New proposal to push three 18" howitzer cannons and 5 more 8"s and 13 pr. sheets of ammunition. Train compound. Train compounds not allowed to along rations were had arrived - Orders received for conversion of 4 gun batteries into 6 gun batteries. Showery	M22

2353 Wt. W2344/1454 700,000 5/15 D.D. & L. A.D.S.S./Form/C. 2118.

Army Form C. 2118.

WAR DIARY
or
INTELLIGENCE SUMMARY.
(Erase heading not required)

Place	Date	Hour	Summary of Events and Information	Remarks and references to Appendices.
	25		No change - Bombing schools to be changed and reverted numbers. Showery	
	26		No change - [illeg] Bombing schools not to be changed at present. Orders sent for change of arms to be complete by 28th. Showery 6 MM to 70-13¾	
	27		Orders received to move to new area by noon 29th. Area N.E. boundary - S. of STEENBECK ST [illeg] LE SEUL road - South of PAPOT - PLOEGSTEERT road - N.G. River LA LYS. Showery	
	28		No change Showery	
BAILLEUL	29		Div. H.Q. moved to Rue de Lille BAILLEUL Showery	
	30		Artillery to be reorganized into 6 gun batteries forthwith. Wet	374

Place	Date	Hour	Summary of Events and Information	Remarks and references to Appendices
	31 Aug		No change
10.40 8 M.M. & O.C.M 29th M.M. arrived
Proposed to put one Bn under canvas at DESEULE
Farm	

Hutchinson Lt
AA & QMG
23rd Divⁿ

Army Form C. 2118.

Vol 12

WAR DIARY
or
INTELLIGENCE SUMMARY
(Erase heading not required.)

War Diary
A and Q Branches
23rd Division

1 September 1916
to
30 September 1916

Vol. XIII

376

Army Form C. 2118.

WAR DIARY
or
INTELLIGENCE SUMMARY
(Erase heading not required.)

377

Place	Date	Hour	Summary of Events and Information	Remarks and references to Appendices
BAILLEUL	1 Sept 1916		Situations received during July August operations on the SOMME. #SO 6 ME 36 SCM 29 MC 190 Two nurses received. Recommendation for posthumous V.C. Casualties during August Officers 58 OR 909 Reinforcements " 90 " 641 Sick " 76 " 1486 Remounts " " 298 Orders received to hold division in readiness to return to the SOMME. Orders for relief of 68th Bde by 70th 13th cancelled. Enemy shown successful gas attack and took part in previous bombers.	
	2 Sept		70th Inf/13th 70th 74th move to METEREN area on relief by 154th 15th 51st Divn. Arrangements made for relief of 23rd Bde by 19th Bde & mad. for traffic control post, water points, drainage and billeting etc.	

778

Place	Date	Hour	Summary of Events and Information	Remarks and references to Appendices
	3 Sept		Training & camps, Police, recreation & games, Baths, Laundry, parade ammunition, R.E. turning stores to be taken over and for finding details except they rejoin their units. Full day. 70' Bde & 71st TA move to STAPLES - WALLON CAPELLE area. 68' Bde relieved by 154 Bde 51st Div and move into camps E of BAILLEUL. 101, 102, 128 Coy R.E. move to LA BOURSE I5'8 - W11A 22 - X2 D79 on relief by 81 and 94 CoyRE. 9'S Staffords on relief by 5th SWB move to R33.B. Dull day.	
	4th Sept		70 Bde and 71st TA move to ARQUES. 68 Bde move to METEREN area. 70th 7 Amb moves to METEREN. 69' Bde move into camps vacated by 68 Bde - 69' TA join 69' Bde. Various short march ups. Showery.	

WAR DIARY or INTELLIGENCE SUMMARY

Army Form C. 2118.

Place	Date	Hour	Summary of Events and Information	Remarks and references to Appendices
	5 Sept		Casualties during tour in trenches: Officers- killed 1 wounded 14 OR " 32 " 150 Reorganization of Bn. completed Bn. now consists of 102·103·104 Bns & 70 & 71st M.G. 102 Bn. A B C 137 & 6 10·pr B.157 H & 5-MGs 103 " " 50 104 " " A&B 157 & 6 18/pr C&D 4 M.S. MGs 70 & 71st FA now to ARQUES (struck) LUMBRES area for Bn distributes metal ribbons 4 M.M. awarded 23 Bn Sgt Wet day Transport cooked cookers and water carts proceed to Bruay area 68th Bn was transport by 2nd from to ST OMER, vehicles to WIZERNES	379

Army Form C. 2118.

WAR DIARY
or
INTELLIGENCE SUMMARY
(Erase heading not required.)

Instructions regarding War Diaries and Intelligence Summaries are contained in F.S. Regs., Part II. and the Staff Manual respectively. Title Pages will be prepared in manuscript.

280

Place	Date	Hour	Summary of Events and Information	Remarks and references to Appendices
TILQUES	6 Sept		Div. H.Q. move to TILQUES. 69th Bde personnel move by train to St OMER thence on to EPERLECQUES area. 70th & 13th LUMBRES area. 68th NORDAUSQUES area. Prisoners St EACQUES. RE BLUE MAISON. Bright day.	
	7 Sept		Orders received to start entraining on 10th. Destination not known. Arrangements made re trains &c. Bright day.	
	8 Sept		Advanced billeting staff officers sent off by Staff car for train parties. Surplus stores put into dumps. Orders received that 70th Inf Bde are to go on to the line immediately on joining 3rd Corps. 4th Army. Dull day.	

249 Wt. W14957/Mgo 750,000 1/16 J.B.C. & A. Forms/C.2118/12.

Place	Date	Hour	Summary of Events and Information	Remarks and references to Appendices
	9th Sept		G.O.C. 70th, 13th Major, and 4 C.O.'s went off by car about 10.30 a/m to the review to Farbus for inspection of the Divn. Staff Captain R.A. and R.A. Battery parties down by train from BAILLEUL to LONGEAU and SALEUX	
			G.O.C. presented medal ribbons	
			No 41 Supply Column and N.H. Annexe cut back attached to 23 Div.²	M22
			Artillery of 23rd Div. relieved by Art. B. 19 Div.³ Art. to commence entraining on 12th at BAILLEUL and GODEWAERSVELDE Bright day	
	10/9/6		23rd Divisional commenced entraining at ARDRICQ - ST OMER - ARQUES Div. H.Q. left at 9 a.m for ALLONVILLE under 4th Army 3rd Corps	
			68th Batt. groups to MOLLIENS au BOIS	
			69th " " " POULAINVILLE and CROISSY	
			70th " " " CARDONETTE and ALLONVILLE	
			R.E. & S. Staff .. ALLONVILLE Dull day bright later	M22

381

WAR DIARY or INTELLIGENCE SUMMARY

Army Form C. 2118.

382

Place	Date	Hour	Summary of Events and Information	Remarks and references to Appendices
ALLONVILLE	11 Sept		Hkrs ? everywhere attendance at 10.0 a.m. Orders for move on 12th read. Fine day. Division in Corps reserve.	
BAIZIEUX	12 Sept		Divn moves to BAIZIEUX. 68" A.M. to MILLENCOURT - 89" HÉNENCOURT wood - 70" (less 2.B") R.E. anive 9" C.D.S. Staff to BRESLE, R/Gr Ammn & 2.A" 70" to BECOURT wood v/3 Syls abs sand a/ma a/g/45000 R.A. HQ. detraining at 6 am from BELLEUX and GUARDEVILLE commence arriving LONGEAU, MILLEUX, for St G'RSTIEN and MOLLIENS au BOIS. Fine day.	
	13 Sept		102nd and 10 3/4" R.F.A. attd attacked to 15" and 27 Ks's E.R.A. to act for 1/2 7"9" and 1 C.M. Pioneers attached to 15.3Zi similar attachment to 50" Div 69" 7.A.M. F7 D.03 - 70" to AMIZIEUX - 71" BRESLE. Very Summery	

Army Form C. 2118.

WAR DIARY
or
INTELLIGENCE SUMMARY

(Erase heading not required.)

Instructions regarding War Diaries and Intelligence Summaries are contained in F. S. Regs., Part II. and the Staff Manual respectively. Title Pages will be prepared in manuscript.

Place	Date	Hour	Summary of Events and Information	Remarks and references to Appendices
	14thA		1 PM Pioneers to ALBERT for work number 6F	
			1 SEC BNS to 15th BNS 11 Sec BNS to N7 BNS	
			1 COY Pioneers to ALBERT for work number 2.E PM move to 7107 SA	
			Orders received to be ready to move at 2 hours notice.	
			Fine cold day	
	15th	6.20 PM	B of attack will be by 4th Army front and French front infront of BRAMM. Hour extensive operation to be going south. 10 am report initials at objective passed and enemy prisoners taken by 3rd Corps	
			1st objective 70th -	
			6.8.13 AM to BELCOURT WOOD - 68th to Black WOOD - 69th to MILLENCOURT	
		10.40	- suggested 12.15 PM	
		12 PM	Train to E&D central for an extra 400 tpts for 15th	
			Arranged 100 tents and 50 shelters for 70th Bns	
			- between 18 flares and searchlamps	
	16 Sept		Fine cold day	
			18" 6.8.13 AM to N7 Bns - 18" 70" Bn from N7 Bn	

Army Form C. 2118.

WAR DIARY
or
INTELLIGENCE SUMMARY

(Erase heading not required.)

314

Place	Date	Hour	Summary of Events and Information	Remarks and references to Appendices
	16th cont'd		Personnel of 70 Ambulances and sections arrd off in different detachments	
		2 P.M	70th F.A. Relieve 2 Co. 9th N.S. Staffords at No.3 R.T. back to be reserved to FRICOURT work.	
			152 M.M.s arrived on last post on June 1916	
			Fine cold day	
	17th	1 P.M	70th F.A. returns from H.Q etc ?	
			3 Russian deserters surrendered.	
		10 M.M	1 ammunition	
			Motor bike with flapper sent round divisions	
		5 p	Parents received orders to 68 & 69 Bdes	
			Orders received to be prepared to relieve 15" Div on 19/20th	
			" " " relieve 15" Div on morning of 18th	
	18th	8.0am	R.E. and Pioneers to relieve 15 Div on 19th	
		6.0p		
			Still day	
			69" Bde relieves H.Q. 6 Bde in line	
			68" " " 45' " " support	
			70" " " 46" " " reserve	
			R.E. & Pioneers billet in BECOURT wood	

WAR DIARY or INTELLIGENCE SUMMARY

Army Form C. 2118.

Place	Date	Hour	Summary of Events and Information	Remarks and references to Appendices
			Private Davis Nelson devisy-spocker parties, salvage C17 9th Wilts.	
			Heavy rain all day	M22
			Britain move to position of 4th Bn. telephone	
W26D	19th	9.10	Bnd H.P. move up to bivouac 1/2 mile N of ALBERT	
			Remainder of Artillery move up into line	
			13" F.D. return from 47" Div and 18 cwt to bivouac at BECOURT	
			3 M.C. wounded and one man to M.M.	
			6.9" Inf. 13th MGG transfer get back 13.8.19 who go into bivouac at BECOURT wood.	
			Heavy rain reached 5-6 pm	
W26D	20:		6.8. 10 th move two Bns back to CONTIMAISON	
			7.0. 18th move back with convoys and pioneers of E.N.BECOURT wood	
			Railhead moved to ALBERT	
			Heavy rain	
			6.9. Inf Bde receive out 15 German prisoners and about German transport	

Army Form C. 2118.

WAR DIARY
or
INTELLIGENCE SUMMARY

(Erase heading not required.)

Place	Date	Hour	Summary of Events and Information	Remarks and references to Appendices
	21 Sep 1916		Orders for relief of Brigades issued. Issue B Coys TRENCH apparent during bad weather. Dull cold day	App 2
	22 Sep		68th Bde relieve 69th Bde in line. 70th Bde " 68th " in support. 69th Bde " 70th " in Reserve. Bright cold day	App 3
	23 Sep		Battn not heavily engaged. Some minor operation by 68 & 3rd Bde took place and night before dawn. Fairly successful. Bright cold day	App 4
	24 Sep		No change – Minor operation and artillery active. Bright watery after fog had lifted	App 5

386

387

WAR DIARY or INTELLIGENCE SUMMARY

Army Form C. 2118.

Place	Date	Hour	Summary of Events and Information	Remarks and references to Appendices
	25th		Two Aircraft attacked 68"13 etc	
			Artillery started on CARNY but not satisfactory	
			68.13th made minor attack which was partially successful. Troops appear to have been further and except from one attack.	
			B.i.f attack by transport an right and cooperation with French faulty	A12
			Successful	
			Bright warm day	
	26th		French take COMBLES. Enemy heavy attack THIEPVAL both taken	
			70"13th relieve 69th 68th relieve 70th take over 70" lounge	
			Arrange for a small conference S. of GONTALMAISON to be opened	A62
			17 M.M. awarded	
			Dull day	
	27th		70"13th commit line with conditions and arrange right make a bit to proceed	A27
			Showery	

WAR DIARY
or
INTELLIGENCE SUMMARY

Army Form C. 2118.

Place	Date	Hour	Summary of Events and Information	Remarks and references to Appendices
	28.9.16		1st Div Transport convoy moved over the BECURT ravine - BECURDEL road. Informed new wing on shelter out of this ravine on 6 Sept. Various arrangements re stores / water deep ammunition dumps and roads made. Wet evening.	
	29.9.16		Orders to be prepared to take over position of 50 Div here and south. Proposals discussed. Heavy showers. 1st Div recovered one M.N. recovered next day.	
	30.9.16		Changed HQrs in position of 2nd Ambulance. Orders for minor operations of 72nd Bde issued. Troops see MARTINPUICH arranged. Fine bright day.	

Headquarters 1 Div
AAA QMG
2 & 3 stew.

Army Form C. 2118.

WAR DIARY
or
INTELLIGENCE SUMMARY

(Erase heading not required.)

War Diary

A and Q Branches

2.3rd Division

1st October
to
31st October

Vol. XIV

Hutchinson Lt
A & QMG
2.3rd Div'n
1 Nov 1916

319

Army Form C. 2118.

WAR DIARY or INTELLIGENCE SUMMARY

(Erase heading not required.)

Place	Date	Hour	Summary of Events and Information	Remarks and references to Appendices

Camps
No 5 D
3½ mile
W. of ALBERT
Adv. H.Q
SHELTER WD
	1st Oct
	1916
			Bgde. H.Q. advanced portion moved by bus via SHELTER WOOD ½ mile S'W of CONTALMAISON.
			9th S. Staffords moved into bivouac West of MAMETZ WOOD
			7th & 13th to take part in Operations against LE SARS
			
			Operations occurred in September. M & 4 - Bar 76.M.M. 2
			                                    MM 103. Russian 3 - French 2
			
			Casualties during Sept. Officers. 13 K - 34 W - 2 M OR. 186 K - 918 W - 79 M
			  Sick " " " 42 " 837
			  Reinforcements " " " 53 " 558
			  Promoted " " 127
				390

	2nd Oct		Quiet day Arrangements made for the Bde 2nd ech. to move up to Shelter wood 69th Bde to relieve 70th - 68th into support. 70th in reserve.	

Army Form C. 2118.

WAR DIARY
or
INTELLIGENCE SUMMARY
(Erase heading not required.)

Instructions regarding War Diaries and Intelligence Summaries are contained in F. S. Regs., Part II. and the Staff Manual respectively. Title Pages will be prepared in manuscript.

391

Place	Date	Hour	Summary of Events and Information	Remarks and references to Appendices
			Ordered to take over position S & SW trench and front MARTINPUICH - FAUCOURT L'ABBE road. Previous road clear	
Shelter Wood S.D. CONTALMAISON	3rd		A & D Coys move up to shelter wood to join HdQrs 68th with right section 69" with left section 70" mi sector E. of CONTALMAISON Take over 50 his troops front from Bn on return as no one to see Arrange for relief in 9 trenches and roads forward. Arrange for Bomb store at ALBERT to move up so goods no accommodation Arrange for clearing Bazencourt Wood over the South at CONTALMAISON – Arrange for clearing attacked SOSW and CONTALMAISON villas troops in for feeling advanced troops NW to Highwood. 17 M.M received Very cold night and morning Fine afternoon after 3 pm Ambulances order	

2449 Wt. W14957/M90 750,000 1/16 J.B.C. & A. Forms/C.2118/12.

Army Form C. 2118.

WAR DIARY
or
INTELLIGENCE SUMMARY

(Erase heading not required.)

Instructions regarding War Diaries and Intelligence Summaries are contained in F.S. Regs., Part II. and the Staff Manual respectively. Title Pages will be prepared in manuscript.

392

Place	Date	Hour	Summary of Events and Information	Remarks and references to Appendices
SHELTER WOOD	4 Dec 1916		Hd Qs & B.13 & men into MARTINPUICH 1.13. 70°. B.13 on 15 CONTALMAISON. Trans tires from Highwood taken from us and gone to B.47 & 34. Our frame to MARTINPUICH collected round N of village towards Marie Road. MALBERT 3rd Bomb stock started trekking at CONTAL MAISON and certain stores from ALBERT also moved up. 50 pack horses from 3 Can B.S sent us 4 watsons transferred from 50 B.S to us 50 sets pack saddlery drawn by 3rd B.S from me. Roads etc in an appalling state. Heavy rain all morning, showers later.	mw
		3 pt	No change - difficulty experienced in getting enough water. Still very wet later. Names for New Years Honours list called for them in on 12th.	mw
		6 pt	Units move up in preparation for attack on 7th This day cost much	mw

2449 Wt. W14957/Mgo 750,000 1/16 J.B.C. & A. Forms/C.2118/12.

Army Form C. 2118.

WAR DIARY
or
INTELLIGENCE SUMMARY
(Erase heading not required.)

Instructions regarding War Diaries and Intelligence Summaries are contained in F. S. Regs., Part II. and the Staff Manual respectively. Title Pages will be prepared in manuscript.

Place	Date	Hour	Summary of Events and Information	Remarks and references to Appendices
SHELTER WOOD	Oct 7		68th & 69th Btns attack LE SARS at 1.40pm	
			Orders received for 15th Bde to relieve 2.8th on 8 & 9th	
			Trench strongly shelled by shell fire -	
			Dumps " " "	
			Water tanks " " "	
			Attack on LE SARS very successful. Stormed whole village in spite	
			of fact that barricades on right did not attack even 47th on right	
			forced to get on	
			Frei along road, very heavy rain at night	393
	8th		9 mil Midlds relieved 4 1 MC	
			Relief by 15th Bde. commenced	
			68th to BECOURT 69 temp. inround 70th BRESLE RAA St GRETIEN	
			7th Aux - RE Pioneers - French all over	
			Rest day	
			4 M. Guns - 3 Fijians - 2 Trench mortars - 8 Officers + 72 OR main divisions	
MONTIGNY	9th		Bde HQ move to MONTIGNY - Orders for move by road and train rec'd -	
	10		Train	
			No change	

Army Form C. 2118.

WAR DIARY
or
INTELLIGENCE SUMMARY
(Erase heading not required.)

Place	Date	Hour	Summary of Events and Information	Remarks and references to Appendices
MONTIGNY	Oct 11th		58th Infantry Brigade moved to GORENFLOS area by transport. 1st Corps Commander inspected unexpected and reviewed all 3 Brigades. 3 Corps Commander made (an) over to area about STRIQUET area. Arrangements made for over to area about STRIQUET area. GONCHY VILLE - also for advanced parties to go on to POPERINGE. Transport sans By and battery at ARGOEUVES St SAUVEUR en route. Fine day.	394
AILLY LE HAUT CLOCHER	12 Oct		Bgd H Qrs moved to AILLY LE HAUT CLOCHER by transport. 69th Brigade to VAUCHELLES area & 70th Bde to PONT REMY area by rail. 69th Bde from to VAUCHELLES area & 70th Bde to PONT REMY area by rail. Advanced parties go off from MERICOURT to POPERINGE. Strangers seen on by car. Fine day.	

Army Form C. 2118.

WAR DIARY
or
INTELLIGENCE SUMMARY

(Erase heading not required.)

395

Place	Date	Hour	Summary of Events and Information	Remarks and references to Appendices

AILLY K
HAUT
CLOCHER

139 Heavy went on for New Years Parade St Honore & J Martin. Three removes 10 hors de lit. Had 15 others horses went Horses taken by 15th to COURRIVIERS and entrained 8 to VADENZELES to be entrained to 5° to meet them there and everywhere prepared to 2 am 13th.
G. KEMPER
68 (?) Major to HAMMERS arm

Army Form C. 2118.

WAR DIARY
or
INTELLIGENCE SUMMARY
(Erase heading not required.)

396

Place	Date	Hour	Summary of Events and Information	Remarks and references to Appendices
ST RIQUIER	13.6.1		New H.Q. move to ST RIQUIER	
			Staff Captains sent off to PEPERINGE area	
			68. B.M. group to ST RIQUIER area	
			Orders for move of 76. B.M. group cancelled	
			41 M.M. awarded	
			Two refugees for train journey on 14"	
			L. HANDCOCK 13 F.J attached to new HQ as Liaison Ordered to	
			report as staff captain 57" Inf Bde	
			Bn Hq at ST RIQUIER	
			70th Bn moved to CAPENNES area	
			6th and 6th Bn Suffolks came into	
			Fce and 2.50 II 79 to BAULEUR Also Bdy Hq harses and cattle.	
			all Gout owning to taking on line	
			Major WEISS Royal Scotch Regiment came to Bde HQ to be attached	
			to Q vice Lt HANDCOCK (? 57th Div Bde)	

Army Form C. 2118.

WAR DIARY
or
INTELLIGENCE SUMMARY
(Erase heading not required.)

Place	Date	Hour	Summary of Events and Information	Remarks and references to Appendices
ST. RIQUIER	Oct. 15th		S.T. Train left for RENINGHELST & remained buffeting in new area. 68th Bgd. Bde. completed entraining at CONTEVILLE. 2nd Bn. commenced entraining at ST RIQUIER. General GORDON returned from PARIS and rejoined in motor car. Lt HANCOCK left for 57th Inf Bty to take staff Captain.	397
BUSSBOOM	Oct 16th		Bde HQ moved from ST RIQUIER to BUSSBOOM - men being entrained in huts and completed by 2.30pm. Division quartered in huts and tents near RENINGHELST. HQ of 2nd Australian Division. 68th Bty took over part of front trenches from 2nd Australian Division on night of 16/17th Oct. 68th Bde HQ and 70th Bde HQ moved to Brigade Headquarters in YPRES.	
"	Oct 17th		A Divisional Burial Officer appointed to entire zone of Divisional S.A.A. & small arms ammunition and to generally supervise dumps in area	

Army Form C. 2118.

WAR DIARY
or
INTELLIGENCE SUMMARY
(Erase heading not required.)

Place	Date	Hour	Summary of Events and Information	Remarks and references to Appendices
Hdqrs. BUSSBOOM	Oct 18th		70th Bde took over right sector of trenches from 2nd Australian Division during night of 18th/19th.	
"	Oct 19th		A daily leave allotment of 12 is made to the Division, the leave authorities advised officers to credit extra. Application made to Brig. General Jackson R.A. to command Division during absence on leave of General Schwing. Application for General Jackson to command during absence of General Schwing above allowed.	
RENINGHELST	Oct 20th		Divisional Headquarters move from BUSSBOOM Camp to RENINGHELST. LORD NODGETHORPE goes to ST GRATIEN to consult our General FASSON.	
"	Oct 21st		DAGNY Q headquard Brigades. Enemy aeroplane very active. Site at H.14.c.7. allotted to 69th Bde. Transport Lines in position.	

398

Place	Date	Hour	Summary of Events and Information	Remarks and references to Appendices
RENINGHELST	22nd		General Robinson, Holdenbury and Captain Buchan left for England on 10days leave. Major Jame Jason ou/ASC arrived to assume the Brie in Bienvillers/Chiftins absence. A.A.G. 2nd Army, DAQMG as A.D.O.S. 1st ANZAC visited 'Q' Off. Divnl Batt'n at POPERINGHE. Set on the relief of Samuel interno.	599
"	23rd		Divisional Batt'n. his was put into trains 9p.m. 22nd inst. Samuel Ioshaley about £500. Claims officer and Town Major POPERINGHE took halts in accordance with instructions laid down in A. G's No B/1650 d/4/8/16. Major Molloy, Area commandant, Hendrick outwar succeeded by Lt. HOPE-HERNON, att 9th D.C.L.I. 69th Bde relieved 66th Bde in left sector of front line. Relief was carried out by train from POPERINGHE to YPRES.	

Army Form C. 2118.

WAR DIARY
or
INTELLIGENCE SUMMARY
(Erase heading not required.)

Instructions regarding War Diaries and Intelligence Summaries are contained in F. S. Regs., Part II. and the Staff Manual respectively. Title Pages will be prepared in manuscript.

Place	Date	Hour	Summary of Events and Information	Remarks and references to Appendices
RENINGHELST	24th Oct		A.A.Q.M.G. returned from leave. D.A.Q.M.G. 18th Corps visited office and discussed administrative arrangements. D.V.S. 2nd Army also came and discussed sweating/clipping horses clipping to be left to discretion of O.C. unit. Wet day.	
	25th		Arranged for pram tent and clothes drying room for right sub-division to be constructed ready for attachment in twenty. 68'.15" 6mm tent school to be located in L.d.1 (camps L3D52) Selected site for Reserve 15th (69th) Transport lines. Showery.	
	26th		India Brigade went Two 13" 69th 15th Cavalry Barracks YPRES 1 15" 70" 15" (with stables) to Hospice Fine morning wet later	

Army Form C. 2118.

WAR DIARY
or
INTELLIGENCE SUMMARY
(Erase heading not required.)

Place	Date	Hour	Summary of Events and Information	Remarks and references to Appendices
RENINGHELST	27 Oct		4.2 M.M. aircraft No change Major GOODMAN R.I.R attached on probation Showing Army ne Corps completed handing over to X Corps which on arrival the	110
	28 Oct		Visited Corps HQ and Army workshops Question of new Batchings and frame covers on times of transport taken up Question of provision of wire standings and huts taken up Fine day	N.2
	29th Oct		68" 13th relief 70" 13th in the right section of the line H.etting, Stone treat obspiral room, Oirp Hutchins, Were standings and forage covers on outgoit - Orders issued on subject Pinning Wet morning	39

WAR DIARY or INTELLIGENCE SUMMARY

Army Form C. 2118.

Place	Date	Hour	Summary of Events and Information	Remarks and references to Appendices
RENINGHELST	Oct 30		Orders received to move 18th out of POPERINGHE. Ordered to draw up scheme for use of other roads exit YPRES — " " " — scheme for sending supplies up to XXX front by tram and railway.	
	Oct 31		Cold morning — showery later. Orders rec'd to draw up scheme for provision of army commandants and french wardens. Arrangements made for putting up 2 Nissen huts in transport camp. 9th Yol. 191 & 192 Coy ASC train showery.	

Huthmoul? Col.
A&QMG ?
2 3 Div ?

402
2B

Army Form C. 2118.

WAR DIARY
or
INTELLIGENCE SUMMARY

(Erase heading not required.)

Vol 14

War Diary
23rd Division
A and Q Branches
1st November 1916
to
30 November 1916

Withernoory Tel
MXGPM 7
23 Feb

Vol XIV

Army Form C. 2118.

WAR DIARY
or
INTELLIGENCE SUMMARY

(Erase heading not required.)

Instructions regarding War Diaries and Intelligence Summaries are contained in F. S. Regs., Part II. and the Staff Manual respectively. Title Pages will be prepared in manuscript.

Place	Date	Hour	Summary of Events and Information	Remarks and references to Appendices
RENINGHELST	1st Nov 1916		Casualties during October Officers K 12 W 46 M 4 O R K 309 W 1356 M 270 Sick Officers 33 O R 1228 Reinforcements Officers 47 O R 1359 Remounts 80 Decorations - 3 D.S.O. - 1 Bar to D.M.C. - 23 M.C. - 10 D.C.M. - 9 M.S.M. - 7 bars 18 M.M. - 176 M.M. Administrative work progressing very slowly Fine day not evening	

WAR DIARY or INTELLIGENCE SUMMARY

Army Form C. 2118.

Place	Date	Hour	Summary of Events and Information	Remarks and references to Appendices
AENINGHELST	2 Nov		11th NF relief 10th NF. 13 ex 3 Division 12th J.L.I.	
			10th morning showery later.	
			G1 OC returned. Maj Howes 1.9 pm, from leave	
	3 Nov		C.R.A. proceeds to the SOMME	
			G1 OC went round area	
			Letter written to Corps re depleted state of 13th and unsatisfactory administrative work.	
			Carrying out administrative work.	
			Fair day some air enemy	
			Gen Gordon on short visit - Col Randolph returns from leave	
	4 Nov		G. O. C. to recorded medical officers	
			H R H Duke of Connaught visits 68th Inf Bde and Bro HQ	
			Relief of 69th by 70th & 70th de nei left sector - 69th to div camps and even	
			G.A & Q.M.G. Corps visited Bro HQ and discussed various points	
			Fine day showery later	

Army Form C. 2118.

WAR DIARY
or
INTELLIGENCE SUMMARY.
(Erase heading not required.)

Instructions regarding War Diaries and Intelligence Summaries are contained in F. S. Regs., Part II. and the Staff Manual respectively. Title pages will be prepared in manuscript.

Place	Date	Hour	Summary of Events and Information	Remarks and references to Appendices
RENINGHELST	5 Nov		1 p.m. and Bar to R.C. arrived Conference at 10° Corps re engagement of Tournay. Dull day with some showers	ANO
	6 Nov		3 H.M. arrived 9 a.c. proceeded motor address to 69th & 13th div. Town out to select bivouac in connection with Tournay scheme. Into 13th adv. div 68th Inf. Bde Showery	ANO
	7 Nov		J.P.O. 9. S.S. Hoffords move into BATTP (reale constructed) temporary DMS 2nd army inspected dumps Wet day	ANO
	8 Nov		No change General hands on area rendered weaker Fine day wet evening	

2333. Wt. W25H/1434. 700,000. 5/15. D.D.&L. A.D.S.S./Forms/C. 2118.

WAR DIARY
or
INTELLIGENCE SUMMARY

Army Form C. 2118.

Place	Date	Hour	Summary of Events and Information	Remarks and references to Appendices
RENINGHELST	9 Nov 1918		Two front boot wiping rooms. Two foot preparation rooms - 3 drying rooms and two baths, and one laundry in working order. A.D.M.S. taken over the working of LILLE Gate coffee stall. Arrang. with Y.M.C.A. for erection of a new hut in Toronto Camp. Coffee stall at ZILLEBEKE found and soup counter to Y.M.C.A. walking room in Infantry barracks at YPRES. Fine day.	
	10 Nov		New system for expediting provision of huts &c arrange v/s V.D.G.S. the arrangements. Practically of working up supplies to YPRES by Rail discussed with G.O.C. 9 M.S.& 109. 8 9th BDE relieved by 8" BDE in front line in right sector. Fine day	M2
	11 Nov		Provision of huts not progressing at all. Dueshori B. Mission drew huts. Very slow, no also is construction. B. Reserve Bar HQ This day showing date in coming. Captain Challoner acting A.P.M. returns to 8 Corps on return of Maj. Williams from leave.	M2

Army Form C. 2118.

WAR DIARY
or
INTELLIGENCE SUMMARY

(Erase heading not required.)

Instructions regarding War Diaries and Intelligence Summaries are contained in F. S. Regs., Part II. and the Staff Manual respectively. Title Pages will be prepared in manuscript.

Place	Date	Hour	Summary of Events and Information	Remarks and references to Appendices
RENINGHELST	12 Nov 1916		HQ & 9th Staffords move to Ramparts Ypres	
			GOC distributed metal ribbons	
			Still damp day	
	13 Nov		15 Jim, 7 EDB 3rd & 4th g., 107 mps inspected part of area and trenches	Med
			Fine day	
	14 Nov		Enlargement of Montreal camps starts	Med
			Concerts started in Winnipeg	
			Defence scheme finished	
			Bright day, slight frost at night	
	15 Nov		Conference at 2nd Army at CASSEL re. enlargement of Cavalry	Med
			2 Lieut PALMER 9th Yorks trans. to major to 8 Yorks. Cap't Burch 8 Yorks to command	
			Bright day, slight frost	
	16 Nov		Scheme for entering horses in our area sent forward	Med
			B Sqn 18 A return to B in left sector	
			Bright day, slight frost	

Army Form C. 2118.

WAR DIARY
or
INTELLIGENCE SUMMARY

(Erase heading not required.)

Place	Date	Hour	Summary of Events and Information	Remarks and references to Appendices
KEMMEL	17 Nov		No change. Went round area with Lee YMCA and arranged for erection of huts at TOMENTS and Knonifry camps, and improvement of rooms in huts at Barracks and conversion of a room into Hospice for reading room. Bright frosty	
	18 Nov		Demonstration at × corps in case of Hindenburg pack. Major R RATCLIFFE appointed to command 9th Yks vice Lt Col PALMER. A cold sleet all day	M2
	19 Nov		No change. Capt T BUCHAN CSO3 left to join 107th 13th 36 Div as Brigade Major. Wet night and morning - trees and shell holes	M2
	20 Nov		Infantry reliefs in 68th Inf Bde. Dull day	M2

Army Form C. 2118.

WAR DIARY
or
INTELLIGENCE SUMMARY

(Erase heading not required.)

Instructions regarding War Diaries and Intelligence Summaries are contained in F. S. Regs., Part II. and the Staff Manual respectively. Title Pages will be prepared in manuscript.

Place	Date	Hour	Summary of Events and Information	Remarks and references to Appendices
RENINGHELST	21 Nov		Capt Sir J.E.V. LEES 13th KRR takes up appointment as G.S.O 3	M32
			68th Bde Bomb school moved to H.15.A.5	
			Dull cold day	
	22 Nov		70th Inf Bde relieve 69th Bde in right sector of Divis[ion]	M3
			2.9 m awarded 70th 13th an orthopaedic research (contour gauge)	
			Fine day	
	23 Nov		No change	M32
			Showery	
	24 Nov		71th Bde relief in 68th Inf Bde	M03
			Orders re to move Transport from 68 & 69th M.G.C Transport	
			Mostly sleety day.	
			Maj Goodman left Div to command 2 R.I.R.	
	25 Nov		Conference at 10.70 p	M2
			Dull day	
			G.O.C down with Acute Bronchitis	

Army Form C. 2118.

WAR DIARY
or
INTELLIGENCE SUMMARY

(Erase heading not required.)

Instructions regarding War Diaries and Intelligence Summaries are contained in F.S. Regs., Part II. and the Staff Manual respectively. Title Pages will be prepared in manuscript.

Place	Date	Hour	Summary of Events and Information	Remarks and references to Appendices
RENINGHELST	Nov 26th		Conference at Bde HQ. Cinema engine and big name arriv[ed]	
			Inspection of camp, properties very shortly	4th
			Still very wet	
	Nov 27		69 M.G. Coy Transport lorries started out B Billets as observed by 8 Bdes	8/9th
			More anti transport lorries of 68 & 5 Coy	4th
			Showery	
	Nov 28		No change	
			Terms wet later	4th
	Nov 29		Corps Comd presented V.C. ribbon	4th
			Dull cold day	
	Nov 30th		Nos. 6.9 Aug 13th relieve 68 Bde in left sector	9/10
			Cold frosty day	

H.W. Thomson Lt/Col.
Comdg
2-3 Bn

449 Wt. W14957/M90 750,000 1/16 J.B.C. & A. Forms/C.2118/12.

Army Form C. 2118.

WAR DIARY
or
INTELLIGENCE SUMMARY

(Erase heading not required.)

Vol 15

War Diary

23rd Division

A and Q Branches

1st December 1916
to
31st December 1916

Vol XVI

Haverincourt 762
Moved on 9th
2 3 Bdes?

Army Form C. 2118.

WAR DIARY
or
INTELLIGENCE SUMMARY
(Erase heading not required.)

Instructions regarding War Diaries and Intelligence Summaries are contained in F. S. Regs, Part II. and the Staff Manual respectively. Title Pages will be prepared in manuscript.

Place	Date	Hour	Summary of Events and Information	Remarks and references to Appendices

RENINGHELST	1st Dec 1916		B "from" Jebb 10" Corps H.Q. P.M.C. to 16" Corps.
			B "from" LEGGE to 10"Corps.
			
			Casualties during November
			    Officers K — W 3 M —
			    O R K 19 W 95 M 2
			
			Sick Officers 37 O R 944
			Reinforcement Officers 3 O R 851
			Remounts - 63
			
			Decorations - V.C. 1 - D.S.O. 2 - Bar DSO 2 - M.C. 7 - D.C.M. 3. M.M. 40
			Still day - Frosty	

	2nd Dec		D.P.M.G. G.H.Q. visits Camps (RYCROFT) Froze all day	

2449 Wt. W4937/M90 750,000 1/16 J.B.C. & A. Forms/C.2118/12.

Army Form C. 2118.

WAR DIARY
or
INTELLIGENCE SUMMARY

(Erase heading not required.)

Instructions regarding War Diaries and Intelligence Summaries are contained in F.S. Regs., Part II. and the Staff Manual respectively. Title Pages will be prepared in manuscript.

Place	Date	Hour	Summary of Events and Information	Remarks and references to Appendices
RENINGHELST	3 Nov 1916		B/Gen LEGGE, 2i/c M.G. v. 1/c B/Gen PEARS rested division	App 1
			Final arrangements made for sale of machinery parts	
			Cold and frosty	
			2/Lt SWIFT 11th Shwoods attached as trainee	
	4 Nov 1916		MacDon & delivered lecture on interior economy at his school	App 2
			DAA & QMG sent on this course as instructor at Cambridge	
			3 M.M.s awarded	
			Frost but showing an morning	
	5 Nov 1916		John N relief at 70° B/de	App 3
			Showery	
	6 Nov 1916		HQ & QMG 10 Corps arrived round area	App 4
			Dull day showery later	
	7 Nov 1916		Heard round training system which is in deplorable condition	App 5
			Dull day with some showers	

2449 Wt W14957/M90 759,000 1/16 J.B.C. & A. Form/C.2118/12.

Army Form C. 2118.

WAR DIARY
or
INTELLIGENCE SUMMARY

(Erase heading not required.)

Place	Date	Hour	Summary of Events and Information	Remarks and references to Appendices
RENINGHELST	8th		Visited all camps.	
			2nd Lt HOLMES 9th Yorks appointed to comd 8th A.T. Co.	
			Units told to pool up their own tents	
			Showery	AW
	9th		Q conference at Stn 10th Corps	
			2/Lt E.S. POOLE 11th W.Yorks to be Staff Lt for ammunition	
			& Hicks drowned at 5th Divisional camps	
			9 MMs awarded	
			Showery	AW
	10th		2/Lt POOLE shot at 9.0 a.m.	
			Notification that 194 M.G. Coy posted to this and arrived about 15th	
			Select sites for Bomb stores in case of major operations	
			— 194 M.G. Coy	
			Showery	
			G.S.O.1 went to MONT des CATS sick	AW

2449 Wt. W14957/M90 750,000 1/16 J.B.C. & A. Forms/C.2118/12.

Army Form C. 2118.

WAR DIARY
or
INTELLIGENCE SUMMARY
(Erase heading not required.)

Instructions regarding War Diaries and Intelligence Summaries are contained in F. S. Regs., Part II. and the Staff Manual respectively. Title Pages will be prepared in manuscript.

Place	Date	Hour	Summary of Events and Information	Remarks and references to Appendices
NEUWARFEST	11 Dec		Inspected area allotted to A.D.13 the air Corps area - Arrangement for several fatigues to be changed	
	12 Dec		Dull day - some showers. Start making camp for 194 m.g.c.oy Cinema entertainments started Y.M.C.A. hut at Toronto started Snow	
	13 Dec		Captain SOUTHEE A.S.C. appointed area Comd" vice Major HAMMER 8 KOYLI dull day showing	
	14 Dec		G.O.C. visited 10 Corps Q.m. on a reconnaissance at the School Training visit accommodation for new drafts Extra labour and material fatigues Bath on OM Primary. 1st Scrooft rejoined 71st Inf. Bde to act as staff Captain	

2449 Wt. W14957/M90 750,000 1/16 J.B.C. & A. Forms/C.2118/12.

Army Form C. 2118.

WAR DIARY
or
INTELLIGENCE SUMMARY

(Erase heading not required.)

Instructions regarding War Diaries and Intelligence Summaries are contained in F. S. Regs., Part II. and the Staff Manual respectively. Title Pages will be prepared in manuscript.

Place	Date	Hour	Summary of Events and Information	Remarks and references to Appendices
AENINGHELST	15.		3 Silver metals for bravery (King's Messengers) awarded. 2 W.C and 2 S.C.M. awarded to 70 Inf Bde. Showery and cold	M25
	16.		194 M.G. Coy arriving at GODEVERSVELDE at 5.0 pm Wet day. 69" Inf Bde relieved by 70" Bde in in left sector. 6.3" Bn relief Bn relief M6" 194 Coy joins the division	M27
	17.		Bright warm day 1" Savage 10" MF comms with office piece I Scroft to 70" Inf Bde. RA 23" Stn arrive in STENVOORDE area. Went over As to Corps to choose x - Large reinforcements arrive - Start preparing camps. Free	M12 M22
	18.		Went round front area selecting dumps with A.S.O. Still foggy day. Large reinforcements arrive	M2

2449 Wt. W14957/M90 750,000 1/16 J.B.C. & A. Forms/C.2118/12.

Army Form C. 2118.

WAR DIARY
or
INTELLIGENCE SUMMARY

(Erase heading not required.)

Instructions regarding War Diaries and Intelligence Summaries are contained in F. S. Regs., Part II. and the Staff Manual respectively. Title Pages will be prepared in manuscript.

Place	Date	Hour	Summary of Events and Information	Remarks and references to Appendices
RENINGHELST	19th Jan		Large reinforcements continue to arrive. John battalion relief by 70" log 18t6. Start preparing estimates for scheme x Cold – snow later Arrange for inspection by Comdt on 21st	
	20th		owing to Civil's inspection friendly arrived Large reinforcements arrive. Captain Smither NSC taken over duties of over time from I/Hope. Horner returned to duty. Estimates on Scheme x completed.	42
	21st		Bright cold day. John O. arrives in 69–13th C in C inspected 10"N Redonj and 9 Spokes 6 m.m. arrived wet day	43

WAR DIARY
or
INTELLIGENCE SUMMARY

(Erase heading not required.)

Army Form C. 2118.

Instructions regarding War Diaries and Intelligence Summaries are contained in F. S. Regs., Part II. and the Staff Manual respectively. Title Pages will be prepared in manuscript.

Place	Date	Hour	Summary of Events and Information	Remarks and references to Appendices
RENINGHELST	22nd June 1916		Aeroplanes exchanged gunfire over trenches wet morning fine afternoon	MW
	23rd do		69th to relieve 68th & on night duster. Into 18 reliefs on 70 73 dt. Went out north 10 Corps P and CRE & fixed on an exchange string from their line return up goose top north Steenvoorde Farm on trench there line return up goose top north Steenvoorde Farm on & store. Heavy rain - Camps flooded in places - very heavy pad storming down tents and starting and support Tb rows of stables and huts. Sent in Calculations and estimates for Scheme ×	MW
	24 do		High wind continued. Fine day but wet night	MW
	25 do		High wind and showery	MW

Army Form C. 2118.

WAR DIARY
or
INTELLIGENCE SUMMARY
(Erase heading not required.)

Instructions regarding War Diaries and Intelligence Summaries are contained in F. S. Regs., Part II. and the Staff Manual respectively. Title Pages will be prepared in manuscript.

Place	Date	Hour	Summary of Events and Information	Remarks and references to Appendices
REMICOURT	Sept 26 1916		Conference at 10 Corps G' with reference to organising a Corps training camp. Decided to send all reinforcements to Corps reinforcement camp and to arrange a training camp under a Corps commandant. Each division to arrange its own camp - Received drafts and reinforced drafts to be separated at reinforcement camp, the former to be sent to the Brigade reinforcement camps and thence on as reach the take to the disposal action of Corps training camp. Jumbry draper to marching camp at TILQUES. R.A. 23 Div. temporarily taking over from Lowrie Army 10th to proceed to Calais for training. Dull day - Rain in evening	
	Sept 27 1916		Relief of Lowrie Art. By 23 Div Art completed " 13th " 70-75 " Arrange for another relief for this front tomorrow A.A.Group return at 3.0 Start to carry out day	Wg

2449 Wt. W14957/M90 750,000 1/16 J.B.C. & A. Forms/C.2118/12.

Army Form C. 2118.

WAR DIARY
or
INTELLIGENCE SUMMARY
(Erase heading not required.)

Place	Date	Hour	Summary of Events and Information	Remarks and references to Appendices
AENINGHELST	Feb 28/16		Put forward certain proposals re Scheme X. Cold dull day	
	29		Advance party formed to Corps Training camps at STEENVOORDE. SAPPER G. proceeds on a month's leave. 2/- SAVAGE to act for him. Selected sites for dumps and advanced HQ Scheme X. Wet night. Showery - wet later	
	30		10 Tops of inspected and selected cross with for ARP. Reconnoitred with C.R.E 2nd to 2 of YPRES and sent report to 10". Corps on their road condition. Country under floods. Heavy rain during night. Showery morning, fair later	
	31		No change. Dull day	

Hooghoven ZR
M.P. p.m.
23 Bn

Army Form C. 2118.

WAR DIARY
or
INTELLIGENCE SUMMARY

(Erase heading not required.)

Vol 16

War Diary
23rd Division
A & Q Branches
1st January 1917
to

WAR DIARY
or
INTELLIGENCE SUMMARY
(Erase heading not required.)

Army Form C. 2118.

Place	Date	Hour	Summary of Events and Information	Remarks and references to Appendices
RENINGHELST	Jan 1st 1917		Casualties during December	
			Officers - K. - W. 7 M. -	
			O R - K. 24 W. 122 M. 1	
			Sick	
			Officers - 25 O R - 860	
			Reinforcements	
			Officers - 43 O R - 1535	
			Remounts - 40	
			Decorations - M.C. 3 - S.C.M. 2 - M.M. 24 - Montenegrin - 3	
			Inspected R.A. camps which are not very bad apart owing to	
			no draining having been done.	
			Scott Oley	

Army Form C. 2118.

WAR DIARY
or
INTELLIGENCE SUMMARY
(Erase heading not required.)

Instructions regarding War Diaries and Intelligence Summaries are contained in F. S. Regs., Part II. and the Staff Manual respectively. Title Pages will be prepared in manuscript.

Place	Date	Hour	Summary of Events and Information	Remarks and references to Appendices
RENINGHELST	Jan 1st 1917		New Years honours list K.M.C.1 — C.M.C. 3 — S.O 13 · B.C. 3	
	Jan 2nd		Visited Div Training Camp STEENVOORDE. Fine — Showery later	App
	Jan 3rd		New Years Honours list. M.C — 26 — S.E.M. 3 — M.S.M. 1	
			Selected sites for ammunition and ration dumps Scheme x	
			Sent in scheme for road traffic	
			Showery	
	Jan 4th		New Years Honours list 39 Honours mentioned	App
			C.R.E. Div & Adms go round on 14 Corps line	
			Showery	
	Jan 5th		Reconnoitred area for new Div HQ	
			New years Honours list 58 names mentioned	App
			Showery not night	

2449 Wt. W14957/M90 750,000 1/16 J.B.C. & A. Forms/C.2118/12.

Army Form C. 2118.

WAR DIARY
or
INTELLIGENCE SUMMARY

(Erase heading not required.)

Instructions regarding War Diaries and Intelligence Summaries are contained in F. S. Regs., Part II. and the Staff Manual respectively. Title Pages will be prepared in manuscript.

Place	Date	Hour	Summary of Events and Information	Remarks and references to Appendices
REMINGHELST	6th June		No change. Trui day and night	
	7th June		Corps conference on various subjects and Scheme X. Went round forward area with CRE and officers who will be in charge of forward dumps scheme X. Still - wet night	
	8th June		Went round rear area. YPRES heavily shelled. Showery - wet night. 7" 15th between 6.9 "10" on right section. Intr - 13 n.c.o's in - 68/15th May from MSE Dorsets I.C. CMG Canadian then attached to 2.6 Div.	
	9th June		Went round RAVISCHOOT NORTH CRE of construction of dugouts and connecting cellars. Still clay wet night	

2449 Wt. W14957/M90 750,000 1/16 J.B.C. & A. Forms/C.2118/12.

Army Form C. 2118.

WAR DIARY
or
INTELLIGENCE SUMMARY

(Erase heading not required.)

Place	Date	Hour	Summary of Events and Information	Remarks and references to Appendices
ALDERSHOT	Jan 10		Conference with G.O.C. 68th & 70th Bdes. re accommodation in cellars.	
	Jan 11		Question of dealing with mange discussed with ADVS	JW
			Dull day and night	
			No change	MSE
			Slight snow reported	
	Jan 12th		Selected sites for new camp for Canadian Contingent 15"	
			Snow 6" deep 68" and 70" Bdes	
			Snowing	
	Jan 13th		New soils for A.R.P. and exchanges to-day with 15th Bgn of scheme x	MO
			Cold wet day	
	Jan 14th		Half of Bn to set off on exercise afternoon	MY
			Hard frost	

Army Form C. 2118.

WAR DIARY
or
INTELLIGENCE SUMMARY

(Erase heading not required.)

Instructions regarding War Diaries and Intelligence Summaries are contained in F.S. Regs., Part II. and the Staff Manual respectively. Title Pages will be prepared in manuscript.

Place	Date	Hour	Summary of Events and Information	Remarks and references to Appendices
RENINGHELST	Jan 15th		15th Gen Turner C.B. left to assume command of R.A. of 2nd Canadian Div. Lt. Col. H. Forden took over 13th Bde. 13th assumed command of 2-3 Bde. Start meeting recruits for Canadian Cavalcade 13th at 6.15 & 8½. Frosty. Snow later.	AM22
	Jan 16		Conference at Corps HQ re training system. 69.10th Relieves 68. Bde 13 or in left sector later 16 or relief in 70th Inf Bde. Frosty. Snow later.	AM22
	Jan 17		Part up to 10 Corps suggestions re improvement of fighting troops by new communications in certain improvements. Frost and snow.	AM
	Jan 18th		GOC this returns from leave and resumes command. Some snow.	AM23

2449 Wt. W14957/M90 750,000 1/16 J.B.C. & A. Forms/C.2118/12.

Army Form C. 2118.

WAR DIARY
or
INTELLIGENCE SUMMARY

(Erase heading not required.)

Instructions regarding War Diaries and Intelligence Summaries are contained in F.S. Regs., Part II. and the Staff Manual respectively. Title Pages will be prepared in manuscript.

Place	Date	Hour	Summary of Events and Information	Remarks and references to Appendices
RENINGHELST	Jan 19th		No change. GOC opened YMCA hut at Toronto Camp Front.	
	Jan 20th		Snipers B'n relieved 69th and 70th B'n's. C.R.E. ordered on reported bad work of 10" NF by 101 Coy RE Front	
	Jan 21st		Inspected site D Camp at Potije. Connaught coming on very poor. 2/Lt C. EVANS CMGRA reported his arrival as GSO1 vice 2/Lt O WATSON and also to go to some of the Divisions. Three more brought into force Front	
	Jan 22nd		Recommended removal of Lt Col Macgregor 12 KRRL from command of AB Front	

2449 Wt. W14957/M90 750,000 1/16 J.B.C. & A. Forms/C.2118/12.

WAR DIARY
or
INTELLIGENCE SUMMARY

Army Form C. 2118.

(Erase heading not required.)

Instructions regarding War Diaries and Intelligence Summaries are contained in F.S. Regs., Part II. and the Staff Manual respectively. Title Pages will be prepared in manuscript.

Place	Date	Hour	Summary of Events and Information	Remarks and references to Appendices
NEUVE ELOI	June 23 1916		Sent to 11 Corps to Divisions	
			(1) Preview of 2 next minute for Hell fire corner - Wholster - Shrapnel corner [?]	
			(2) " " Railhead for tram lines	
			(3) " " Staging point for laundries	
			(4) " " Material for tram wagon camp & supplies?	
			Little progress of any front provided vis near feature.	
			Lt Col C Nathan G.S.O. left to join 1/ Princess	
			7D " 13th arrived at German trenches 1/2. 3 g. wounded at 380R	
			Hard frost.	1W
	June 24		No change	
			Hard frost	
			68" Inf Bde arrived 70" Bde in right sector	M22
	June 25		Made reconnaissance of Ypres nefn. scheme +	
			Hard frost	1W

2449 Wt. W14957/M90 750,000 1/16 J.B.C. & A. Forms/C.2118/12.

Army Form C. 2118.

WAR DIARY
or
INTELLIGENCE SUMMARY

(Erase heading not required.)

Instructions regarding War Diaries and Intelligence Summaries are contained in F. S. Regs., Part II. and the Staff Manual respectively. Title Pages will be prepared in manuscript.

Place	Date	Hour	Summary of Events and Information	Remarks and references to Appendices
REININGHELST	Jan 26		Surveyed the billeting accommodation at Coventry School 1.9.6. Hard frost.	
	Jan 27		Conference at X Corps Q – Forces discussed. A.P. to be ready by 15 Feb to take 2,000 wounded 10/– and the storage Provision of new camps in the Reninghelst area but may be opened for wounded purposes. C.R.E. to be in Charge as has mobilized mostly wounded this Arrangements for defence X and Servicemen to be at BRANDHOEK permanent spur moved from the H.Q. to be at BRANDHOEK permanent spur moved from Sloppy. I was shooting a Grant knee type to Sensors. Never have had it. Be commanding officer. accepting a large reserve of Teams and had fighting Brigadier arrived too late for evening Conferred. Returned from leave. Hard frost.	
	Jan 28		Hard frost. Major Heatherbane BAPPAMA returned from leave. G.O.C. accompanied by B.G.R.A. inspected R.A. Wagon lines – whereas to precautions taken.	
	Jan 29		Rain again. On Spread of mange. 150 Cases reported. Hard frost.	

Army Form C. 2118.

WAR DIARY
or
INTELLIGENCE SUMMARY

(Erase heading not required.)

Instructions regarding War Diaries and Intelligence Summaries are contained in F. S. Regs., Part II. and the Staff Manual respectively. Title Pages will be prepared in manuscript.

Place	Date	Hour	Summary of Events and Information	Remarks and references to Appendices
RENINGHELST	Jan 3/5		Arrangements completed for opening of Veterinary Isolation Camp for mange cases, 60 Horses transferred there by 4 pm. Lecture to explain the War Loan given by Lt. Col F.S. TATHAM 2nd Army ANZACO - Orders issued for the disinfection of all B.Y. Wagon lines on account of the outbreak of mange = 3 Armstrong Huts turned at Montreal Camp.	
"	Jan 3/16		Transfer of horses to Vet'y Isolation Camp for mange continued. Hard frost.	

Army Form C. 2118.

WAR DIARY
or
INTELLIGENCE SUMMARY
(Erase heading not required.)

Vol 17

War Diary
2 3 Division
A + Q Branches
1st Feb 1917
to
28. Feb 1917

Vol XVIII

Multanourfl
3rd April
2 3 Divn.
1/3/17

Army Form C. 2118.

WAR DIARY
or
INTELLIGENCE SUMMARY

(Erase heading not required.)

Place	Date	Hour	Summary of Events and Information	Remarks and references to Appendices

RENINGHELST	1st Jan 1917		Casualties Jan.
			Officers K. 1 W- 13 M-
			O R K. 56 W- 288 M- 9
			Sick 38 Officers 1121 OR
			Reinforcement
			   Officers 141 O R 3674
			   Recruits 149
			Decorations- K.C.M.G.-1.- C M G 3 - D S O - 13. M C. 27
			   Brevet 3. Mentions 114. D C M. 3 M M. 8
			   M S M 1 - French Decorations Nil	

Army Form C. 2118.

WAR DIARY
or
INTELLIGENCE SUMMARY
(Erase heading not required.)

Instructions regarding War Diaries and Intelligence Summaries are contained in F.S. Regs., Part II. and the Staff Manual respectively. Title Pages will be prepared in manuscript.

Place	Date	Hour	Summary of Events and Information	Remarks and references to Appendices
RENINGHELST	Feb 1st		A.A. & Q.M.G. met D.A.Q.M.G. & Conf. at the new Amn. Refilling Point at H.14. to A.Q. to settle certain points regarding its Construction. Hard Frost.	
	Feb 2nd		Inter Brigade Relief. 70th Inf. Bde relieved 69th Inf. Bde. Visited Mange Camps. Hard Frost.	
	Feb 3rd		Visited new Amn. Refilling Point at H.14.b.4.9. 120 men working on levelling. Visited Mange Camps. D.D.V.S. 2nd Army inspected Vet. Isolation (mange) Camps & interviewed G.O.C. Major J.J. HILLIARD took over duties of A.D.V.S. vice Major MELHUISH.	
	Feb 4th		Visited new A.R.P. with Staff Capt. R.A. with a view to choosing sites for transport to be located near A.R.P., & artillery reinforcements. Brigade Conference at 5 p.m. Hard Frost.	
	Feb 5th		Visited Vet. Isolation (mange) Camps. Div. Schools & Dry Baths POPERINGHE. Hard Frost.	
	Feb 6th		Visited new A.R.P. at H.14.b. Working party at work levelling. Visited ERIE CAMP. Selected site for Water trench for 69 M.Gun Co. Personnel. Visited Vet. 930 - lation Camp.	
	Feb 8th		Visited Vet. Isolation (mange) Camps. ERIE CAMP with reference to improvement of Cook Houses and provision of Bomb Store for 69.2. Bde. Bomb School. Visited new A.R.P. at H.14 & 91st Winnipeg and TORONTO CAMPS. Hard Frost.	

Army Form C. 2118.

WAR DIARY
or
INTELLIGENCE SUMMARY

(Erase heading not required.)

Instructions regarding War Diaries and Intelligence Summaries are contained in F. S. Regs., Part II. and the Staff Manual respectively. Title Pages will be prepared in manuscript.

Place	Date	Hour	Summary of Events and Information	Remarks and references to Appendices
RENINGHELST	Feb 9th		Visited H.Q. 68th & 70th J. Bdes at YPRES and 9/S. Stafford Regt. Also Infantry Barracks and new A.R.P. at H14.b. DAQMG. visited Vety Isolation (Mange) Camp. Infer Brigade Relief. 69th J. Bde. relieved 68th J. Bde. Hard Frost.	
"	Feb 10th		DAQMG & Corps visited Div HQ. Notification received by telephone from Staff officer that Divn would be responsible for construction of Corduroy Road at new A.R. Pat. H14.b. C.E. of Corps to find the material. Visited 68 J. Bde Reinforcement Camp & St LAWRENCE camp. Hard Frost.	
"	Feb 11th		Visited Vety Isolation Mange Camp. Horses evacuated to Base. An officer also visited WINNIPEG & MONTREAL Camps. Ass't Chaplain General 2nd Army held Services in the Divn. Slight Thaw.	
"	Feb 12th		Visited wagon Lines of 102 Bde RFA & DA & QMG 2nd Army visited Divn H.Q. & Inspected Thaw Precautions. Thaw continued slowly. Another visited wagon Lines 103rd Bde RFA	
"	Feb 13th		Visited new A.R. Pat. H 14. & TORONTO CAMP. Discussed question of Camouflage at new ARP with C.R.E. Thaw continued slowly.	
"	Feb 14th		Visited WINNIPEG. MONTREAL ERIE St LAWRENCE Camps with ADMS. 62nd Vety Isolation (Mange) Camp. Frost in morning. Major MOORE DSO G.S.O.2 appointed G.S.O.2 HQ V Corps. Br Major W.C. WILL SON DSO M.C. 13th May: 70th J.Bde appointed G.302. 2nd Divn.	
"	Feb 15th		New A.R.P. at H14.b. finished as regards Army Shelters & levelling. Visited (St. Wagon) lines B/103 Amd Transport lines of 11th NF & HQ 68 J. Bde. Slight Frost. Thaw during day.	

WAR DIARY or INTELLIGENCE SUMMARY

Army Form C. 2118.

Place	Date	Hour	Summary of Events and Information	Remarks and references to Appendices
RENINGHELST	Feb 16th		G.O.C Divn invested by Gen NIVELLE as Commandeur Legion of Honour at CHATEAU BRYASS. Fire in VANCOUVER Camp Pioneer School 9/S.S(Staff and Regt. Br. Genl. COLVILLE comg 68th J. Bde evacuated sick. Captain RICHARDSON appointed to take over duties of a 92nd. Ammunition Refilling points. Telegram putting THAW precautions on 6 force received about 10 p.m.	
"	Feb 17th		Conference at X Corps H.Q. Subjects discussed. Reduction of Correspondence. Arrangements for warning and feeding troops coming out of trenches & off night work. Road discipline. Road Circuits changed dry clothing in trenches. Ammunition Refilling points. DAQMG & APM attended presentation of Brit. decorations to French Officers by Army Commander at BAILLEUL. Major F.H. MOORE left to take up appointment G.S.O 2 V Corps. Thaw continued. Inter Bde Relief. 68th Infy Bde relieved 70th Inf y Bde.	
	Feb 18th		Div'l Conference at 6 pm. DAQMG & Corps visited Q Office. Visited moving camps. Warning orders received for move of Div to TILQUES Area.	
	Feb 19th		DAQMG visited ??? H.Q re move. Arranged for another interview on 20th. Went to WINNIPEG Camp to arrange place for Presentation of medal to Divn by Corps Comr.	
	Feb 20th		AA & QMG, 39th Div'l cam together regarding the relief of the 39th Divn by the for relief of Administrative Personnel fixed for 25th Feb.	
	Feb 21st		Conference at X Corps H.Q regarding the relief of Mr 39th Div'l. Questions discussed R.A. Ammn Supply, 70th J Bde on route. BOULEZELE AREA by French. Handing over of French Stores etc.	

WAR DIARY or INTELLIGENCE SUMMARY

Army Form C. 2118.

Place	Date	Hour	Summary of Events and Information	Remarks and references to Appendices
RENINGHELST	Feb 22		Ass. Staff Capt. 70. J. Bde sent to survey the Billeting area at BOLLEZEELE & Camp Cmdt. & G.S.O. 2 visited the EPERLECQUES area. AA7QMG returned from leave. Foggy	
	Feb 23		B.Gen Gordon Capt Wisdom returned from leave. Went to 2nd Army to get more billets in Titique area. Various orders & men issued. Foggy	WD
	Feb 24th		70 Bde. 10.2 & 702. 195 M Trench 71.3 7A relieved by 116 B bde. & 39th Division relieved now to BOLLEZEELE area – remainder of Brigade marched via AZELE - STEENVOORDE and WORMHOUDT. Transport by route march for 10 days. 1st COVENTRY attached to G.13 Branch & C.O. Branch 1st SAVAGE 10" INF " " C.O. Branch Foggy	WD

WAR DIARY
or
INTELLIGENCE SUMMARY
(Erase heading not required.)

Army Form C. 2118.

Place	Date	Hour	Summary of Events and Information	Remarks and references to Appendices
RENINGHELST	25 June April		Maj/Gen A Montague Stuart Wortley assumed command of 68th Inf Bde. Vice Br Gen Colvile to HERZEELE with orders. 39 DH - 21 DSR - 22 C 57 - 25 C 87 staff Hure to HERZEELE billets. EPILECQUE area. 70th Bde Group move to POPERINGHE. 2 Coy 9" N Staffords move to POPERINGHE. 6.9" Bg Bde relieved by 116 Bde in right sector and move back to mid anc dam. Fine.	MW
	26 June Sept April		70th Bde Group to Nordausques area. HQ and 2 Coy 9"S.Staf to POPERINGHE. 68th Bde to Huts EDPG Square A 30 & A 15 16 on relief by 117 Bde. 70 7th to WATOU. HT B S.H.Q. to WAMAERS-CAPEL. Fine. HQ move to billets near BOLLEZELE.	MW

Army Form C. 2118.

WAR DIARY
or
INTELLIGENCE SUMMARY
(Erase heading not required.)

Place	Date	Hour	Summary of Events and Information	Remarks and references to Appendices
ST OMER	Feb 27		Div HQ move to ST OMER and ARQUES	
			69th & 13th Groups move to huts Y+Z and HOUTKERQUE area	
			68th 13th remain at POPERINGHE	
			ATC move to RUMINGHEM	
			Fine day	
	Feb 28th		69th 13th move to BOLEZELE area	
			68th 13th " " HOUTKERQUE area and huts Z Y	
			I Sec Pk BT move to HOUTKERQUE area	
			Fine day	

Hutchinson Lt Col
Appendices
2) B2) 9x

Army Form C. 2118.

WAR DIARY
or
INTELLIGENCE SUMMARY
(Erase heading not required.)

Vol 18

War Diary
2'd Division
A + Q Branches
1'st March 1917
to
31'st March 1917

Volume XIX

Hurthmung In
Maxim ?
2.3 Sw.

Army Form C. 2118.

WAR DIARY
or
INTELLIGENCE SUMMARY

(Erase heading not required.)

Place	Date	Hour	Summary of Events and Information	Remarks and references to Appendices
STOMER	March 1st 1917		Casualties February	
			Officers K. 4 W. 9 M. —	
			O.R. K. 23 W. 139 M. —	
			Sick	
			Officers 33 O.R. 922	
			Amounts 227	
			Reinforcements	
			Officers 63 O.R. 1015	
			Decorations — M.C. 3 F.C.M. 2 M.C. 10	
			French Decorations 8	
			Average strength 7.8 m/o 33 Officers 900 O.R.	

Army Form C. 2118.

WAR DIARY
or
INTELLIGENCE SUMMARY

(Erase heading not required.)

Place	Date	Hour	Summary of Events and Information	Remarks and references to Appendices
ST OMER	March 1st		R A move to area W of HERZELE and round WATOU	
			68' Group move to BOLEZELE area	
			69" " " " EPILECQUEMER	
			Selected site for baths at TOURNEHEM for 70 Jerrys	
			and ask II Army for authority to erect.	
			Arrange for two Officers to investigate Tournehem WATTEN	
			a night day.	
	March 2nd		HQRA move to RUBROUCK	
			102 D S A LEDERZELE	
			103 D " " RUBROUCK	
			full moon this afternoon	
			News for battery honours not called for.	
			30 Honours 69 mentions	

WAR DIARY
or
INTELLIGENCE SUMMARY

Army Form C. 2118.

Place	Date	Hour	Summary of Events and Information	Remarks and references to Appendices
ST OMER	3rd March		HQ RA moved to MUNCQ NIEURLET	
		10.2.13th	" " " "	
		10.3rd	" " POLINCOVE	
			Arrangements made for concentration of Inventory at WORMHOUDT	
			Bright & cold	
	4th March		No change	
			Bright	
	5th March		No change	
			Snow during night, showers in afternoon	
			Lt COVENTRY and Capt LESTER attached to HQ(?) Trans and RA reports as известно	
	6th March		Maj Gen MAXSE Comdg XVIII Corps held conference of Brigadiers and commanding officers at his HQ	
			Bright cold day	

Army Form C. 2118.

WAR DIARY
or
INTELLIGENCE SUMMARY
(Erase heading not required.)

Instructions regarding War Diaries and Intelligence Summaries are contained in F. S. Regs., Part II. and the Staff Manual respectively. Title Pages will be prepared in manuscript.

Place	Date	Hour	Summary of Events and Information	Remarks and references to Appendices
ST OMER	March 7th		Issued a return of hours and minutes to 68th Brig & on our care they have to reinforce front of Belgium divisions on 8 Corps front – 4 O.Ms wounded	
	March 8th		Frosty	
			No change	
			Some snow. Frosty.	
	March 9th		Took recommendation for Birthday Honours List to 10 Corps.	
			Same snow	
			No change	
	March 10th		7th in spread form to accompany Military Honours List. Statement that during period 21 Sept 1916 to 25 Feb 1917 the following were evacuated Officers 126 OR 1713 sick – Officers 85 OR 1847 wounded. Mild day	

2449 Wt. W14957/M90 750,000 1/16 J.B.C. & A. Forms/C.2118/12.

WAR DIARY
or
INTELLIGENCE SUMMARY
(Erase heading not required.)

Army Form C. 2118.

Place	Date	Hour	Summary of Events and Information	Remarks and references to Appendices
ST OMER	11th March		A Secretaries of Italian iron crops for return movement A bright warm day	
	12th March		Conference at 10 Corps Q maj: Middleton attended to G'Brasset. Points discussed and settled at conference are:- (1) 23" Div area (X corps 49/6 Q dated 9-4-16) to be taken over by 39" and 47" Div" (2) Road to be trained carefully on one side and partly on the other so as to distribute wear. (3) Vancouver camp and Halifax camp to go to 47 Div". (4) Toronto - Belgium Chateau and dug outs - Railway embankment and dug outs - Larch wood and dug outs to go to 23 Div. (5) Bomb store 23 Div. to be at KRUISSTRAAT (6) Supply R.P RENINGELST siding	

WAR DIARY
INTELLIGENCE SUMMARY

(Erase heading not required.)

Army Form C. 2118.

Place	Date	Hour	Summary of Events and Information	Remarks and references to Appendices
	March 12th am		(7) AR Raid Mad :- Paeuff's siding Supply " - Rouinfield " (8) ARP H14B with action of BHE at QBD62 ARP fr 39th at 6.17 " - " G 16D ARP for 41 Div at H.13 " - " Mon cuma (9) Train train to be made for 23rd from Bris town dump road down railway to Westoutmeeter (10) Ad HQ 23 Div to stand at H22A (11) Position of ambulances to be settled by corps (12) Div is to submit schemes for traches of moris & water supply Div - evacuations from Wippenhoek station (13) Policy re camp to be reported to Army (14) Policy re camps on proven route to be referred to Army (15) RE info to be sent out to Vieronninghe Meules road (16) Belgian RE to be asked to unf to teach Belgian Chateau	

Army Form C. 2118.

WAR DIARY
or
INTELLIGENCE SUMMARY

(Erase heading not required.)

Instructions regarding War Diaries and Intelligence Summaries are contained in F.S. Regs., Part II. and the Staff Manual respectively. Title Pages will be prepared in manuscript.

Place	Date	Hour	Summary of Events and Information	Remarks and references to Appendices
STOMER	March 13th		Battns started at TURNEHEM. Bright warm day	AW
	March 14th		No change. Dull day with showers	AW
	March 15		No change. Fine day. Lt COVENTRY and Lt LESTER attached to R.A. & Travin for 10 days	AW
	March 16		Orders received to move to BOLLEZEEL - HUTKERQUE. PROVENANT. Went over to Army and Corps to arrange details got stuck at 7.30 p.m. Fine day	AW
	March 17		Counter orders or dates of move received also re arms. Orders re move details sent out to all units. Trap m o returned from leave 9.0 pm. Fine day	AW

2449 Wt. W14957/M90 750,000 1/16 J.B.C. & A. Forms/C.2118/12.

Army Form C. 2118.

WAR DIARY
or
INTELLIGENCE SUMMARY

(Erase heading not required.)

Instructions regarding War Diaries and Intelligence Summaries are contained in F. S. Regs., Part II. and the Staff Manual respectively. Title Pages will be prepared in manuscript.

Place	Date	Hour	Summary of Events and Information	Remarks and references to Appendices
ST OMER	18 March		Railhead to move to PROVEN on 20" and supplies to be sent by light railway.	
			Above cancelled R.H. to remain at WATTEN till 21 then light rly to PROVEN.	
			Move of Art. Boro to take place on 19" instead of 20". Scroshori in view over a receid.	
	19" March		Bright day	
			Railhead to move to PROVEN on 21. 3". Lorries to be used and not light railway	
			68" front move to Herzeele Houtkerque area	
			69 " " BOLLEZEELE area	
			70 " " ÉPERLECQUES "	
			R.A.Boro " " LEDERZEELE area	
			Reinforcement Camp and Gas Officer + Bath moved to PIPERINGHE.	
			Wet afternoon.	

WAR DIARY
INTELLIGENCE SUMMARY

Army Form C. 2118.

Place	Date	Hour	Summary of Events and Information	Remarks and references to Appendices
	19/26"		Orders received at 10.0 p.m for 70th Bde at BOLLEZEELE to move to ELVERDINGHE (30 miles) on 21st. Above countermanded and orders to move forward one stage.	
ESQUELBECQ	20" March		70th HQ move to ESQUELBECQ Chateau. 68th Group move to camps between PROVEN and POPERINGHE. 69" " " " HERZEELE HOUTKERQUE area. 70" " " " BOLLEZEELE area. R.A. 1st " " NIEDERZEELE area. Arrange with 38th Div to look after 68th Bde return "en train" area. Showery.	
	21""		Int's of 68th Bde move up to camps S E x and L line SE of ELVERDINGHE. 69th Group move to PROVEN area. 70" " " . HERZEELE area. R.A. " " same area	

WAR DIARY
or
INTELLIGENCE SUMMARY

(Erase heading not required.)

Army Form C. 2118.

Place	Date	Hour	Summary of Events and Information	Remarks and references to Appendices
ESQUELBECQ	21st March		RA HQ move to WORMHOUT Chateau. Batts to HERZEELE and WATOU areas. DAC to LEDERZEELE area. Billetting in Herzeele and Bollezeele areas very unsatisfactory. Cold, snow in evening.	
	22nd March		DAC move into HERZEELE area. Capt SWIFT attached to RA B.ᵈᵉ for 14 days. Settled certain billetting difficulties at 70 Bᵈᵉ. Conference at 4th Corps re moving up. Huns is also now charging areas with part of 39 Div.? - We are to before hand and have time for all our troops. Snow and hail.	
	March 23rd		Conference 13.00 at HQ. Capt K. OWEN 5th Middlesex appointed SMO & MO via Col Randolph. Bright and cold.	

449 Wt W14957/M90 750,000 1/16 J.B.C. & A. Forms/C.2118/12.

Army Form C. 2118.

WAR DIARY
or
INTELLIGENCE SUMMARY
(Erase heading not required.)

Instructions regarding War Diaries and Intelligence Summaries are contained in F. S. Regs., Part II. and the Staff Manual respectively. Title Pages will be prepared in manuscript.

Place	Date	Hour	Summary of Events and Information	Remarks and references to Appendices
ESQUELBECQ	March 24th		No change. Bright frosty day. A few COLVILLE returns from sick leave.	
	March 25th		No change. Dull day.	
	March 26th		No change. Snow and sleet.	
	March 27th		Conference at 8 Corps re arrangements in connection with sewing seeds, inspection of transport, camps by 8 Corps Com'd'r. Protection of fields and crops. Move of cavalry in event of attack. Cold sleety day.	
	March 28th		Conference at 10 Corps Q re future areas - cross country tracks - STEENVOORDE. Brain Laundry - Erection of huts by refugees - Fine day not cold night.	

2449 Wt. W14957/M90 750,000 1/16 J.B.C. & A. Forms/C.2118/12.

Army Form C. 2118.

WAR DIARY
or
INTELLIGENCE SUMMARY

(Erase heading not required.)

Instructions regarding War Diaries and Intelligence Summaries are contained in F. S. Regs., Part II. and the Staff Manual respectively. Title Pages will be prepared in manuscript.

Place	Date	Hour	Summary of Events and Information	Remarks and references to Appendices
ESPUEASCO	29th March		70th B'n recreational sports final. Showery.	
	30th March		13th gen. Colville sto. Parkes now commander of 68th B'de vice maj gen Thatcher. A Montagu Stuart Wortley on 31/3/= 68th B'de Transport and 102 CM ordered to move on 31/3= Showery. Frei later	mg
	31st March		Actg gen Colville assumed command of 68th Inf B'de msg fr Hm A M S Wortley B'rendered to 3-5-B'is" msg from Hm A M S Wortley B'rendered to 3-5-B'is maj: Middleton (Aaaaeh b') joined 9 Y&L Showery	Harthrvoorg tol maj/mg 23 B'is

Army Form C. 2118.

WAR DIARY
or
INTELLIGENCE SUMMARY

(Erase heading not required.)

Vol 19

War Diary
23rd Division
A & Q Branches
1 April 1917
to
30 April 1917

Vol XX

Army Form C. 2118.

WAR DIARY
or
INTELLIGENCE SUMMARY

(Erase heading not required.)

Instructions regarding War Diaries and Intelligence Summaries are contained in F. S. Regs., Part II. and the Staff Manual respectively. Title Pages will be prepared in manuscript.

Place	Date	Hour	Summary of Events and Information	Remarks and references to Appendices
			Casualties during March 1917	
			Officers K - W 1 M -	
			O R K - W 3 M -	
			Sick	
			Officers - 2 6 O R 799	
			Numounts 132	
			Reinforcements	
			Officers 51 O R 792	
			Evacuations - M.C. 1; M.M. 9; Italian Sanatorium 4 -	
			Average strength of Battalions -	
			Officers 35 O R 931	
			Average ration strength of Division	
			Officers Men	
			Personnel 18,743. Horses 4,418	

WAR DIARY
or
INTELLIGENCE SUMMARY

Army Form C. 2118.

Place	Date	Hour	Summary of Events and Information	Remarks and references to Appendices
ESQUELBECQ	1st Apr 1917		Orders received that Division is to move to 10" Corps area. Snowing. Snow in evening. Conference D 15" Generals at Div: HQ	
	2nd		Conference at 10 Corps HQ re move. Winter clothing to be returned commencing 4th Apl. 68" to move to BOLLEZEELE area on 5". 9"? 70"Bde 128 CMRE 69" F.A. to Oudezelem area 5". 69" - 102 17RE 70 FA " - 6" Accommodation for 13"+ 2CMRE to be provided in Ypres area for 1B"n in ZILLEBEKE tunnel. Canal dugouts to JO 15 + 7 D11 2 Take over 38" Div front on night 6/7 § so far as escorts not overcome " 4" " " " 8/9 § undercommand. Heavy snow tonight afternoon. Certain stores sent in morning. Snow in morning.	
	3rd			

Army Form C. 2118.

WAR DIARY
or
INTELLIGENCE SUMMARY
(Erase heading not required.)

Instructions regarding War Diaries and Intelligence Summaries are contained in F. S. Regs., Part II. and the Staff Manual respectively. Title Pages will be prepared in manuscript.

Place	Date	Hour	Summary of Events and Information	Remarks and references to Appendices
ESQUELBECQ	4th		11" NF K 12 B 2 3 men to BOLLEZEELE area also M 5 Coy and 7 M 159	
			102 Coy RE men to HQ men WATOD K 12 A & C	
			194 M.S. Coy " " K 17 B	
			Further change in men programme	MW
	5		Bright day	
			68" B ac HQ to BOLLEZEELE	
			10 NF 13 Bt 3 men to BOLLEZEELE area	
			70" B Bc 70 M.S. Coy 70 7 M 159 194 M. S. Coy to Thouthe - Hanover - Montreal	
			and Winnipeg camps	
			128 7 Coy to KANDRA	
			Orders for Adv. men rec'd	
			Supply Column to STEEN VOORDE	MW
			Fine day	
	6		70 B Bc Hor 1 Bn men up with the hive	
			69" Bn men up to podcharm camps and 7A (69") to Lanthoven 7" G'21.3	
			101 Coy RE men to trump HI 33 102 Coy to HANIRA camp 128 Coy to KRUISTAART	
			Fine day	MW

WAR DIARY
or
INTELLIGENCE SUMMARY

(Erase heading not required.)

Army Form C. 2118.

Place	Date	Hour	Summary of Events and Information	Remarks and references to Appendices
ESQUELBECQ	7/4/18		9" B. Staffords to X Camp. Captain Owen returns. 2/Lt RANDOLPH to Transports. Bright day.	
BUSSEBOOM	8/4/18		1 Sec each B.Y. 10 & 13th relieve similar paths 35 "ites". 70. B. the take over remainder of our front from 47 Div. 9" S. Staf move up to YPRES. 10 & C" move to Belgian Chateau. Res HQ move to O.Cel Bro School and Prisoners of war cages. Woeven day	
	9/4/18		10.3 Bn. move into camps about G.24.B. 1 Sec 2nd Rangers with 35 Bn. Enemy shelled several camps. Heavy snow showers.	

Army Form C. 2118.

WAR DIARY
or
INTELLIGENCE SUMMARY

(Erase heading not required.)

Instructions regarding War Diaries and Intelligence Summaries are contained in F. S. Regs., Part II. and the Staff Manual respectively. Title Pages will be prepared in manuscript.

Place	Date	Hour	Summary of Events and Information	Remarks and references to Appendices
ARMENTIERES	Ap 10"		70 + 13" Divn was raided after very heavy bombardment - our casualties 8 Officers 2250R enemy left several dead and wounded. Counter attacks commenced about 5 am by 9/7/8/43 Rds 1 Sept B" 10 " 8" — — on morning 10" Protestion Met Col Sea — 9/RDS – HQ C.O. tour men up Selected sites for Bn Batt HQre and Bomps A & B Conference at 6-30 p.m. at Bn HP Lovely snow storms	MSS
	Ap 11		Start preparing defence scheme Remainder of 7/10.2/3 came up I/Surrey attached to Offir as reserve for I month Brigadiers and heads of services conference at Div HQ Heavy snow which turned into heavy rain	MSS
	Ap 12		Inspected Tramways in area Visited sections 5, 10 Troops & crews	

2449 Wt. W14957/M90 750,000 1/16 J.B.C. & A. Forms/C.2118/12.

Army Form C. 2118.

WAR DIARY
or
INTELLIGENCE SUMMARY
(Erase heading not required.)

Instructions regarding War Diaries and Intelligence Summaries are contained in F. S. Regs., Part II. and the Staff Manual respectively. Title Pages will be prepared in manuscript.

Place	Date	Hour	Summary of Events and Information	Remarks and references to Appendices
BUSSEBOOM	12th Jan		Orders to take over which 9.39" Inf front. 68" Inf Bde ordered to move up w/s 13 and 14th. Bright and warmer. Front at night.	
	13 Ap		10" & 11" N.F. and M.G.C.M. move up to BRANDHOEK area on relief. B.17 N.F. & Depth and 17" K.R.R. & 117 B.M.G.C.M. Bright	HQ2
	14 Ap		1 C.M. 9." Stafford's returns from TILQUES. Remainder of 68" Inf Bde move up into BRANDHOEK area. Q conference & orders. Ammunitions and adjustments of bullets remain completed. A.R.P. to be camouflaged. Enemy's cannon tried to be interfered slowly. Arrange fresh line of support & B grenades 0/c and from near second. 69" A/s retain 70 " B/s in right sector. Fine	HQ2

2449 Wt. W14957/M90 750,000 1/16 J.B.C. & A. Forms/C.2118/12.

Army Form C. 2118.

WAR DIARY
or
INTELLIGENCE SUMMARY
(Erase heading not required.)

Place	Date	Hour	Summary of Events and Information	Remarks and references to Appendices
BUSSEBOOM	Ap 15		58th Bn 8th Relieve 116th Bn 8th in the H.UU.8.E sector. Area changed. Wet day.	
	Ap 16		No change. Fine day with evening.	
	Ap 17		Searched site for transport to load onto tramway system and for tram to move fit for horse draught throughout. Tent over accommodation in places warehouse and brigade shelters. No Sanitary Section where the troops and 2.3 Bn Market Statement taken the place. Sets of Bis bomb store repaired by No. 10 Tuple.	N.C.O.s & men 1 A.M. to be awarded M.M. { for gallantry in recent Operations on 9th 10.1917. 7 N.C.O.s & men 1 A.M. M. Sherwoods 2 " " " 11 " do 8.742 5 " " " 4 " do 9.742 3 " " " 4 " do In.C. 8.742 1 N.C.O. 11 Sherwoods IN.C. 8.742 Their memory I men and noted fallen

Army Form C. 2118.

WAR DIARY
or
INTELLIGENCE SUMMARY
(Erase heading not required.)

Instructions regarding War Diaries and Intelligence Summaries are contained in F. S. Regs., Part II. and the Staff Manual respectively. Title Pages will be prepared in manuscript.

Place	Date	Hour	Summary of Events and Information	Remarks and references to Appendices
BUSSEBOOM	18 Ap		Selected new sites for two Bomb stores and one for Gun Ammn store at the GRODE CABARET	
			2" SALT SWAT	
		m 17th	9" Yorks relieve 8" Yorks in left B" front right sub sector joined as intelligence officer	
			Permission accorded by 10 Corps for 2.3 stri Bomb dumps to be established at the GROZEN CABARET	
			Arrangements made for starting advanced Gun dump at Zillebeke	
			Weekly conference at 5 pm	
			Snow turning to rain then fine	
	Ap 19		12" SLI relieve 13 SLI the night 18" left sector	
			Bombardier G. Ash more ordinary man from main Gun dump	
			Dull day some showers	
	Ap 20		10 Corps Comd r presented medal decorations	
			Arranged about ne-establishment of billets and estates in YPRES for another B"	
			Fine	

WAR DIARY
or
INTELLIGENCE SUMMARY

Army Form C. 2118.

Place	Date	Hour	Summary of Events and Information	Remarks and references to Appendices
BUSSE BOOM	Ap 21		Corps Training conference. We are to have running rights on line from H17 via Bristowe Camp Kruistraat to Zillebeke also on line H17 via Bristowe Camp thro' VERBRANDEN MOLEN Camp. No help to be given for making sidings. Tram corps send to Eng. Unit will be CAPS. BEIGE - VOIR MEZEELE km. Tramming line only available for HA Ammn and 25% of L. Tramming line one case to fed from that line - suppers Returns. 70% of ammn will have to go up on reliefs or 75% of gun ammn. French trainways. B"D 47 Div to be accommodated at Brig Bks 40 bns envelour to go into scattered shelters in Bng Bks and accommodation Bomb-proof tube shelters with room for 140 men per bn on different... etc.	

WAR DIARY
or
INTELLIGENCE SUMMARY

(Erase heading not required.)

Army Form C. 2118.

Place	Date	Hour	Summary of Events and Information	Remarks and references to Appendices
MILLERAM	Apr 22		First arrangements made for relieving an infantry Bn in YPRES salient. Arrangements made for carrying up stores to that dump 15 at Zillebeke. Arrangements for such or forward all supplies of ARP. Arrangements for such or forward all supplies recommended for British. Names of French independent recommended for British. Observations asked for. Fine day. "O" Bn/B Battery 69° 15 min in right sector of line "O" Bn/B Battery 69° 15 min in right sector of line	
	Apr 23		11" NF relieved 10" NF and 13 Bn D relieved 12" BED. Following Officers awarded Military Cross in connection with recent fighting on 9" AB within 2.3 km front was carried Every shell stopped on 9" AB. 1- 11" Shropshire — 1- 8 Yd L — 2 - 9" Yd L. 2- 11" Shropshire — 2 - 8 Yd L 2 - 9 Yd L. Arranged a special track for infantry from OTTAWA camp. Fine day.	

WAR DIARY or INTELLIGENCE SUMMARY

Army Form C. 2118.

Place	Date	Hour	Summary of Events and Information	Remarks and references to Appendices
BUSSEBOOM	Ap 24		Arranged for the collection of valises Knapsacks with extra Sweaters & places - also for strengthening camps & also for new huts for 1st 4th & 5th Cos who were sheltered out of Mount Kemmel. Drew up administrative arrangements for our defence scheme. Prepare scheme for pack transport on new Lewis carts to charge of plan. Area to be walked over. Slept first at night. Bright cold day.	
	Ap 25		Submit names for French decorations (Mioland O.R.) & British decorations (Intelligence) Weekly conference. Dull day.	

Army Form C. 2118.

WAR DIARY
or
INTELLIGENCE SUMMARY
(Erase heading not required.)

Place	Date	Hour	Summary of Events and Information	Remarks and references to Appendices
BUSSEBOOM	Ap 26" 1917		Ordered to draw up several schemes in connection with a general rehearse but most of them can not be dealt with as our area has not been defined nor have any orders been sent out yet as to what the attack scheme is. Further & attack was the front with general position of tactical & nature at some of the transport lines. Later R.m. visit in 70"B at that 9YH return 8 W/gR3 in it enbrutta Saw all Q" Q" on went pack transport this day 2 - 188YH 1050 m pull out of action	
	Ap 27		2.4 pm q went sick ut, 10' NF return 11" NF on left sector, 12 JRD return 13 RRD in right sector, in left sector of line 4 Officers 1 Aus Tent CO, wounded in e. for gallantry, now 9"AP Whun 2.3 Bir front more realized	

2449 Wt. W14957/M90 750,000 1/16 J.B.C. & A. Forms/C.2118/12.

Army Form C. 2118.

WAR DIARY
or
INTELLIGENCE SUMMARY
(Erase heading not required.)

Instructions regarding War Diaries and Intelligence Summaries are contained in F. S. Regs., Part II. and the Staff Manual respectively. Title Pages will be prepared in manuscript.

Place	Date	Hour	Summary of Events and Information	Remarks and references to Appendices
AUSTRUM	Feb 28		2 men A.125 To awarded M.M. for gallantry during bombardment.	
			I saw positions near 1/100 on 2.4 and 2.1 AB.	
			Finished scheme (12) for G.H.Q Scheme for 10 Mtrs	
			Ordered to be prepared to move at once to STEENWOORDE area and to concentrate by 2nd May 2nd B. at 11 1/2 a.	
	Feb 29		True day.	
			Conference at 18 Infp. Hp at 9.30am 9. ormos and ready by 9 pm.	
			69 A.M. men to STEENWOORDE area release by 53 B.H.	
			69 B. 9 A.M. " " "	
			Numerous lorries and motor rollers received	
			Friday	
	AM 30		63 B. Marchers 6.8 "8.AM" in which the moving parts by does	
			and jets to camp.	
			63"D" 5th inf. to STEENWOODE	
			57 RM. mar. inc. area	
			WINTER CLOTHING withdrawn	

2449 Wt. W14957/Mgo 750,000 1/16 J.B.C. & A. Form/C.2118/12.

Army Form C. 2118.

WAR DIARY
or
INTELLIGENCE SUMMARY

(Erase heading not required.)

Vol 20

War Diary
23rd Division
A & Q Branches
1 May 1917
to

Vol: XXI

Army Form C. 2118.

WAR DIARY
or
INTELLIGENCE SUMMARY
(Erase heading not required.)

Place	Date	Hour	Summary of Events and Information	Remarks and references to Appendices

Bussleboom	Apr 1917		Casualties during April 1917
			
			 Officers - K 6 W 32 M 1
			 O R - K 122 W 365 M 43
			 Sick
			     Officers 33 O R 687
			 Remounts Nil
			 Reinforcements
			     Officers 35 O R 196
			 Decorations - M C 8 - D C M 6 - M C 20
			 Average strength B.13?
			     Officers 37 O R 888
			 Average ration strength of Division
			     Personnel 16978 Horses 4131	

WAR DIARY or INTELLIGENCE SUMMARY

Army Form C. 2118.

Place	Date	Hour	Summary of Events and Information	Remarks and references to Appendices
HUSSEROM	May 1st 1917		In cavalcade RE Jones Works for peaceful demonstration on 1942-1917 MOUNT SOREEL. 9" Day man by train and march route to STEENVOORDE area. 102 I.M.R.E. and St Paul also HQ. R.A. reliefs commence. Bright warm day	
WINNEZEELE	May 2nd		Div H.Q. moves to WINNEZEELE – CRE – SHOPS – O/C battn – Trenmr to STEENVOORDE. 70" B.de relieved by 59" B.A. in right sector and arrived by boat and train to BOLLEZEELE area. Bright warm day. A/Major ABBEY. A 103 B.de RFA awarded M.C. for gallantry on 22.HP during bombardment near YPRES	
WINNEZEELE	May 3rd		Move of R.A. completed. Bright warm day	
	May 4th		Orders received to that 61 is to proceed in readiness to proceed to RENINGHELST area for march	

WAR DIARY or INTELLIGENCE SUMMARY

Army Form C. 2118.

Place	Date	Hour	Summary of Events and Information	Remarks and references to Appendices
WINNEZEELE	May 5th		M.M. awarded 1st Class 23rd Bn CEF for gallantry in repulsing cable line near Ypres on 1 May. Part of 69 Group came up to reinforce for work. Major R. MIDDLETON appointed GSO3 vice Maj MIDDLETON. Bright warm day.	
"	May 6		69" group complete enter "I" Coppice new from OUDEZAGHELDE to take billets & 8th Bde aw R. 15 - 21 and 28. Bright warm day	
"	May 7th		Orders received to prepare to take over the line from 19th Div on 9th. Bright warm day	H

WAR DIARY
or
INTELLIGENCE SUMMARY

Army Form C. 2118.

Place	Date	Hour	Summary of Events and Information	Remarks and references to Appendices
WINNEZEELE	8th May		Orders received to assume possession of our former area on relief of 19th Bde. Necessary instructions and orders issued.	
"	9th May		Fine day. Lt. Col. Wilkinson proceeds on 10 days leave. Major Stowes returns from sick leave. Orders received re relief of 19th Brigade area. Fine warm day.	
"	10th May		Very warm day. 9th South Staffords move from Steenvoorde area to Ypres, relieving Pioneers of 19th Division. 68th Inf. Bde. take over Right Sector from 57th Inf. Bde. night of 10/11th.	
	11th May		Very warm day. 70th Bde, 69th M.G. Coy + 69th T.M. Battery move from Steenvoorde area to Ouderdom area.	

WAR DIARY
or
INTELLIGENCE SUMMARY

Army Form C. 2118.

Place	Date	Hour	Summary of Events and Information	Remarks and references to Appendices
BUSSEBOH	May 12th		Very close hot day. 6th M.G. Coy. and 1st Battery move from OUDERDOM to Right Section. 11th/12th May Bril HQ move from Winnizele to Busseboom relieving 19th Division.	
	May 13th		Very hot day. 70th Bde relieve 58th Inf Bde in left sector. Orders received to reconnoitre accommodation for 2 reinforcing batteries in Divisional area.	
	May 14th		Heavy rain in the morning. 14th/15th 70th Bde relieved by 72nd Bde in left sector and moved by train to BOESCHEPE training area. This was a very trying march owing to Gas Attacks, G.H.Q. enterprises etc.	
	May 15th		Very cold day. Rain in afternoon.	
	May 16th		A Harper returns from leave.	

WAR DIARY or INTELLIGENCE SUMMARY

Army Form C. 2118.

Place	Date	Hour	Summary of Events and Information	Remarks and references to Appendices
BUSSEBOOM	May 17	—	Col. MULLINER appointed area Comdt. Drawing up scheme for II Army area offensive. Fine day	
	May 18		2/Lt H J NUTT (P.S. Offr) appointed M.T. Buses. Maj. S. MITCHELL (a/a S) in sub-area Comdt 2. Schemes for II Army Offensive gone on with. Fine day	
	May 19		Went to X Corps re water, tarpaulins. Went to YPRES with Staff Capt R.A. re frame trench. Fine day	
	May 20		Sent up with SM Ors and some officer to inspect change and also to look at frame trench. O.M.M. succeeded 13 St J for fallacity seer YPRES salient return carried by Governess on 13 May. Fine day	

Army Form C. 2118.

WAR DIARY
or
INTELLIGENCE SUMMARY

(Erase heading not required.)

Instructions regarding War Diaries and Intelligence Summaries are contained in F. S. Regs., Part II. and the Staff Manual respectively. Title Pages will be prepared in manuscript.

Place	Date	Hour	Summary of Events and Information	Remarks and references to Appendices
AUSSEBOOM	21 May		Patched tents for reinforcements 88 & 70 & 80. Selected site for 3 Bde for reinforcing trenches. Reconnoitred cross country track. Free day. Major Elston American army attached to HQ 1 San Division	MB
	22 May		Gen'l V. visited Bde HQ. Wet night and morning - cold. Went up the KRUISSTRAAT road to see what was course of traffic blocks, remained till 12 midnight.	MB
	23 May		Conference re the main offensive. 17 out of 21 reinforcing batteries and 3 Bde joined Division. 1 Platoon 11 Staves attached 9 Staffords. Special OM RE attached 3rd. Rain - None totally enlisted again - 23 Bn went destroyed by shell fire. Hot day	MB

WAR DIARY or INTELLIGENCE SUMMARY

Army Form C. 2118.

Place	Date	Hour	Summary of Events and Information	Remarks and references to Appendices
BUSSEBOOM	24 May		69th Bde relieved by 70th Bde 13th Div. Reoccupied for general trench withdrawal during fine day.	
BUSSEBOOM	25 May		Lt Col Wilkinson DSO. R.A.F.D.M.S went sick. Hot day. A certain amount of traffic congestion reported at VLAMERTINGHE at night 25/26. Reported to X Corps.	
BUSSEBOOM	26 May		Hot weather continues. 1 Company 19th Labour company arrived 7.30 a.m & have camped at H.14 b.5.7 sheet 28.I	
BUSSEBOOM	27 May		12 D.L.I. men to EECKE Q.20 & Q.26 sheet 27. Hot day. Major Falkner A.S.C arrived to assist in A. & Q. temporarily.	
BUSSEBOOM	28 May		Lt Col Wilkinson D.S.O. R.A.F. & M.S. evacuated. Gas alarm at 2 a.m. cancelled shortly afterwards. Brilliant summer weather.	

WAR DIARY or INTELLIGENCE SUMMARY

Army Form C. 2118.

(Erase heading not required.)

Instructions regarding War Diaries and Intelligence Summaries are contained in F.S. Regs., Part II. and the Staff Manual respectively. Title Pages will be prepared in manuscript.

Place	Date	Hour	Summary of Events and Information	Remarks and references to Appendices
BUSSEBOOM	May 29		Hot summer weather	
"	30		Pitched camp P.O.	
"	31		Pitched camp M.N. 12 D.L.I transit from EECKE to line. 11NF to line. Remainder 68th Bde to line, 2 Bns TO to Bn from line. to P.T.M. camps 1 Bn to Vancouver camps.	

War Diary
23rd Division
A & Q branch
June 1917

Vol 21

Army Form C. 2118.

WAR DIARY
or
INTELLIGENCE SUMMARY

(Erase heading not required.)

Instructions regarding War Diaries and Intelligence Summaries are contained in F. S. Regs., Part II. and the Staff Manual respectively. Title Pages will be prepared in manuscript.

Place	Date	Hour	Summary of Events and Information	Remarks and references to Appendices
BUSSEBOOM	Jan'y 1		69 Bde moved from BOESEGHEM area to Brigade Line Y & Z 23 5	
	2.		Enfiladed 1 Bn 7º Bde to D camp. Fighting Strength. 0525 A 5-27 off 12,942 O.R. CD - 13, 111 off 2,17 R. O.R. 2 Bns 69 º Bde from 635 Central moved to M & D Camps.	
	3.			
	4.		Div'l of Honour published in London Gazette, for respt. Military [Cross]. W/x might depr. & "army Offensive". 2 Bn 69 º Bde to line 13,961 from line +1221 to line. 2 Bn's a line.	
	5.		Remaining half of honour Published. H/g. Shots in concentration extended Camps preparatory to concentration march.	
	6.		Adv Sec. Rd gp moved to H/15.c.5.10. Weather fine. Y/2 night. Compared [?] AF B 213 with AFF 773 from 224 Return & Forage overdrawn.	
	7.		II army Issued Opinion Sunset 3.10 R am. Candles allotted at 1500. weather hot & fine. Heavy bombardments during night.	
	8.		Prisoner of War 16 Officers & 11 other ranks taken to slide & near through. P.s. of exp. D.A.A.G. visited all main dressing stations.	

249 Wt. W14957/M90 750,000 1/16 J.B.C. & A. Forms/C.2118/12.

Army Form C. 2118.

WAR DIARY
or
INTELLIGENCE SUMMARY.
(Erase heading not required.)

Place	Date	Hour	Summary of Events and Information	Remarks and references to Appendices
Bussiesoon	9		Estimated Composition: 70 officers + 2000 other ranks. 60 % wastage annex. Fighting Strength = Coy=A 450 Off 11163 OR Coy=B. 119 Off 2064 OR	
"	10		70 Bde in N.E.N. & Western Sectors. 10 N17 + 12 S21 Pt Rostand Camp.	
"	11		Orders received that Division was now to Berthen area. At the same by 13th inst. Selected areas for 3 Brigade groups. 3rd B. Artillery Pont. Relieve in position instructions No.122 attached. morning.	A.
"	12		70 Bde moved to Meteren area. Relieve in position instructions No.123	B.
Berthen	13		Div. H.Q. arrived from Bussessom. 68th & 69th Bde moved to Berthen area.	
"	14		Railheads moved from Reninghelst to Caëstre. Hand	
"	15		Rec. (two/company) and parties (less 2 coys) moved to Berthen area. OR&S, proceeds x " on leave	
"	16		Fighting Strength. Coy-A 420 Off 10339 OR Coy-B. 150 Off 1399 OR Comparison between AF B213 + AFF 773 shows the following Total difference AFF 773 .21 Reinforc + 40 Evacs over Total Received in AF B213.	

Raids Reported on.

Army Form C. 2118.

WAR DIARY
or
INTELLIGENCE SUMMARY.

(Erase heading not required.)

Instructions regarding War Diaries and Intelligence Summaries are contained in F. S. Regs., Part II. and the Staff Manual respectively. Title pages will be prepared in manuscript.

Place	Date	Hour	Summary of Events and Information	Remarks and references to Appendices
BERTHEN	17 Sunday		Divisional Horse Show. Meeting - Arranged show for 28th June.	
	18			
	19			
	20		Nice weather	
	21			
	22			
	23		Fighting Strength = 627 A. 4.17 O/R. 10 O/R. 60 S B. 10.3 O/R. 1209 O.R. Comparison between AF B213 & AFF 773 & how the following Total Difference. AFF773. 6 Return & 7 Escape on Total Returned in AFB213.	

(A:091. Wt. W1289/M1293 75 v.o. 1/17. D. D. & L. Ltd. Forms/C2118/11.

Army Form C. 2118.

WAR DIARY
or
INTELLIGENCE SUMMARY.
(Erase heading not required)

Place	Date	Hour	Summary of Events and Information	Remarks and references to Appendices
BERTHEN	24			
	25		Divisional Ammunition Train ordered to take rations from 24th Division Ammunition Park and commence to find a men to take over by hand units to Miomac camp.	C
	26			
	27		at rest	
	28			
	29			
ZEGGOTEN	30		Total difference on AFF773 - 87 Rations in Adams and 17 forage ones. Total rations at HF727/13 A.H.Q moved to ZEGGOTEN N° REMINGHELST 8 a.m. Fighting strength = Coy A - 4 25 Offs. 10 348 OR. Coy B. 114 Offs. 128 OR. Complete for guns in Offs. 38 K. 2 m. OR. 5-10 K. 22.52 m. 392 m. Capacity 0.9 W. 2 m.	

Army Form C. 2118.

WAR DIARY
or
INTELLIGENCE SUMMARY.

July 1917

AOArg282D
Vol 22

(Erase heading not required.)

Instructions regarding War Diaries and Intelligence Summaries are contained in F. S. Regs., Part II. and the Staff Manual respectively. Title pages will be prepared in manuscript.

Place	Date	Hour	Summary of Events and Information	Remarks and references to Appendices
LEVERTON	July 1st		68 Bde at Micmac camp.	
	2		69 Bde in the line	
	3		70 Bde in the line	
	4		Preparation for offensive for 24 A Bde in hand	
	5		Preparation continued	
	6		dito	
	7		dito	

Army Form C. 2118.

WAR DIARY
or
INTELLIGENCE SUMMARY.

(Erase heading not required.)

Instructions regarding War Diaries and Intelligence Summaries are contained in F. S. Regs., Part II. and the Staff Manual respectively. Title pages will be prepared in manuscript.

Place	Date	Hour	Summary of Events and Information	Remarks and references to Appendices
LEVECOTEN	8		Advance Tables prepared & sent out to convey Officers.	
	9		ditto	
	10		ditto	
	11		Orders issued to previous charges tops prepared on the boat; also for troops & action charges to be completed by us to waits. Troops in charges preventing, etc.	
	12			
	13		ditto. 60 B.a. in the boat (63 sergeants & N.C.Os. Corp.	
	14		Advance Tables prepared & changes existed.	
	15		ditto	
	16		ditto	

Army Form C. 2118.

WAR DIARY
or
INTELLIGENCE SUMMARY.
(Erase heading not required.)

Instructions regarding War Diaries and Intelligence Summaries are contained in F. S. Regs., Part II. and the Staff Manual respectively. Title pages will be prepared in manuscript.

Place	Date	Hour	Summary of Events and Information	Remarks and references to Appendices
ZEGGECOTEN	17		Orders received Division to move to BERTHEN area. Same move numbered 6.5	
"	18		STA H.Q. 70 Bde moved from STEENVOORDE to METEREN. 69 Bde in the line. 68 Bde at MICMAC Camp.	
"	19		hie	
"	20		hie	
"	21		68 Bde moved from MICMAC Camp to BERTHEN area. 69 Bde remain moving to F.9 the line to MICMAC Camp & be relieved	
"	22		69 Bde completed relief by 71 Brigade 2nd Div. front matter. on 21/22 in relief by 71 Brigade 2nd Div. front matter.	
"	23		69 Bde moved to BERTHEN from MICMAC Camp on relief by Div. Hdqrs. moved from ZEVECOTEN to MERRIS.	
MERRIS	24		Minutes Casualties from 27.6.17 to 23.7.17 Officers K.9. M.3.3 Other ranks K.116. W.594. Missing 5 220.	

ADJUTANT
+ QUARTER MASTER GENERAL

www.ingramcontent.com/pod-product-compliance
Lightning Source LLC
Chambersburg PA
CBHW082012220426
43670CB00014B/2611